ITALO-CANADIANS
Nationality
and Citizenship

D0830655

ESSENTIAL ESSAYS SERIES 63

**Canada Council   Conseil des Arts
for the Arts   du Canada**

**ONTARIO ARTS COUNCIL
CONSEIL DES ARTS DE L'ONTARIO**

an Ontario government agency
un organisme du gouvernement de l'Ontario

Guernica Editions Inc. acknowledges the support
of the Canada Council for the Arts and the Ontario Arts
Council. The Ontario Arts Council is an agency
of the Government of Ontario.

We acknowledge the financial support of the Government
of Canada through the Canada Book Fund (CBF)
for our publishing activities.

Co-Published with Centro Scuola e Cultura Italiana

ALBERTO DI GIOVANNI

ITALO-CANADIANS

Nationality and Citizenship

PREFACE BY
Odoardo Di Santo

INTRODUCTION BY
Errico Centofanti

GUERNICA
TORONTO • BUFFALO • LANCASTER (U.K.)
2015

Michael Mirolla, general editor
Guernica Editions Inc.
1569 Heritage Way, Oakville, ON L6M 2Z7
2250 Military Road, Tonawanda, N.Y. 14150-6000 U.S.A.

FRONT COVER IMAGE MOSAIC MURAL
LOCATION: Piazza della Fontana Mary Bartolini @ Villa Colombo, 40 Playfair Ave, Toronto
ARTIST: Alexander von Svoboda, born in Austria in 1929
INSTALLATION: 1975 by Connolly Marble and Mosaic, Olvino De Carli family
SPONSORED by: Colombo Lions Club
OWNER/COPYRIGHT: Villa Charities Inc…all rights reserved

Distributors:
University of Toronto Press Distribution,
5201 Dufferin Street, Toronto (ON), Canada M3H 5T8
Gazelle Book Services, White Cross Mills, High Town, Lancaster LA1 4XS U.K.

First edition.
Printed in Canada.

Legal Deposit – Third Quarter
Library of Congress Catalog Card Number: 2014957591
Library and Archives Canada Cataloguing in Publication

Di Giovanni, Alberto, 1945-, author
Italo-Canadians : nationality and citizenship / Alberto
Di Giovanni.

(Essential essays series ; 63)
Includes essays originally written in English and not previously
published in the author's Italo-Canadesi.
Includes bibliographical references and index.
Issued in print and electronic formats.
ISBN 978-1-55071-915-4 (pbk.). – ISBN 978-1-55071-916-1
(epub). – ISBN 978-1-55071-917-8 (mobi)

1. Italian Canadians – History – 20th century. 2. Italian
Canadians – History – 21st century. 3. Italian
Canadians – Ontario – Toronto – History – 20th century.
4. Italian Canadians – Ontario – Toronto – History – 21st century.
I. Title. II. Series: Essential essays series (Toronto, Ont.) ; 63

FC106.I8D59 2014   971.004'51   C2014-904180-2
                                              C2014-904181-0

To my wife Caroline
our children Carlo Alberto, Franca, and Annamaria
and our grandchildren David Alberto and Grace Elisabetta
with love

Contents

Foreword

IN WRITING THIS BOOK I tried to follow the lesson of the dramatist and poet Bertolt Brecht: "History is made by people, by many people, and not few." To have a vision of micro-history it is necessary to examine specific events and places, to emphasize the contribution of the common people. These events, places, and people have a name. For this, the reader will encounter many names, names of people of our own time, to prove that we do not need to seek refuge in the past to claim our role. We live history every day, largely without being aware of it.

Gino Ventresca, Fred Zorzi, Bruno Mesaglio, Isa Scotti, Maria Grifone Bandiera, Oreste Cerbara, by their lives, examples, and achievements form an essential part of our history. In proofreading this book, I became aware of how often I referred to myself, and I'm somewhat embarrassed by this. However, upon reflection, I have to accept the fact that I have simply related my own professional life and experience, and in so doing my story provides firsthand testimony to the larger events that unfolded in my community, and the Canadian society that provided the context. I belonged to a generation known for its social and cultural engagement, full of ideals and dreams, some real, some impossible to achieve. This was the driving force of our lives. For this reason, I hope the readers will understand and forgive me.

I also find it necessary to account for another peculiarity, though one I had foreseen even before starting to write. In this volume I make reference almost exclusively to events and activities in Toronto. I had no choice, since Toronto has been the place where most of my life experience occurred. Toronto is one of the major factors in the life of the Italian community in Canada, and as such it surely provides a mirror of the wider experience of the post-war Italian Canadians.

Finally, I have to fulfil an obligation which is also a great pleasure, since we are talking about gratitude, one of the most beautiful gifts we can cultivate in life. I want to express my sincere thanks to those who have encouraged me to write this book, aware that I will certainly notice I have missed quite a few, once the book is in print. First of all, my sincerest thanks to my wife Caroline, for her gracious intellectual support along with her attention to our daily routines.

Thanks to Errico Centofanti, Antonia Serrao-Soppelsa, and Odoardo Di Santo for their editorial assistance, their trust, and their continued friendship. Thanks also to Domenico Servello, the new Director of Centro Scuola, for his steady support as a colleague for 20 years.

ALBERTO DI GIOVANNI
Toronto
November, 2014

Preface

MANY BOOKS have been written on Italian immigration, in many different styles: memoirs, recollections, historical analysis of particular aspects, sociological analysis, in general, all giving prominence to *memory*.

Differing from previous publications, and with a wider scope, Alberto Di Giovanni, founding director of Centro Scuola e Cultura Italiana, has harvested his memories into one volume, *Italo-Canadians: Nationality and Citizenship*. The result emerges as a wide panorama of the recent history of Canada and its social development, while offering a fascinating account of the long journey of the Italian community in Canada, together *with* Canada.

Distinct from so many other memoirs, Di Giovanni creates a picture of the Italian Canadian community drawn from his personal experience as an attentive observer, but above all an active participant in the events that characterized the development of the Italian community, especially in the initial phases of post-war settlement, driven by the massive waves of immigration in the 1950s and `60s.

In that onslaught, the Italian Canadians battled to survive in a land quite different from Italy, in language, customs, climate, and traditions. These were the years when the Italian Canadians became aware of their own ability. From this point, they began the long path towards integration into the major institutions of labour, education, politics, religion, and social life.

Di Giovanni proceeds with great intuition, offering the readers an emerging picture of Canada, illustrating the structure, history, and social evolution that, in a relatively short time, went from being a country of "hewers of wood and drawers of water" to an industrial nation, included in the club of the most advanced countries, the so-called G8.

Di Giovanni arrived in Canada in 1963, joining the numerous family members who had preceded him. In relating his personal experience as a young immigrant, he tells the story of Canada. His first contacts were with the university; the various organizations of the community; the world of labour; and the emerging union organizations his brothers were involved with. He came to understand the conditions facing the children of immigrants in the sometimes hostile school environment. Thus he saw the necessity of getting involved in the teaching of Italian (and the other third languages) by establishing the Centro Scuola e Cultura Italiana which, after 40 years, remains an outstanding example of a brilliant success.

Di Giovanni, the unrepentant optimist, at the end of a career that "wasn't short and wasn't easy," says he is satisfied because he has seen that "we Italian Canadians have acquired that status of citizenship and nationality which doesn't in the least diminish the full recognition of our Italian roots. We can take pride in having achieved with intelligence and honesty the right of being acknowledged as authentic citizens of Canada."

Offering an analysis of the nature of immigration to Canada chapter by chapter, Di Giovanni examines with clear and concise language the various aspects of the Canadian reality, in conjunction with his personal experience and that of many other Italian Canadians. In this framework, he examines the phenomenon of multiculturalism and its positive evolution, notwithstanding the opposition from the strong lobby for the status quo, reflecting the permanent duality of Canadian society. It was forged originally from the two dominant groups, Francophone and Anglophone, deliberately in contrast to the politics of the melting pot in the United States. The aboriginals, in spite of being the original Canadian population, have always been pushed to the margins, and to this day are still excluded from the chambers of power.

An important chapter is dedicated to the evolution of our community, burdened in the uncertain beginning by the bothersome presence of notables and aspiring notables that Di Giovanni calls "wannabes," up to the initial stages of organizations such as FACI and the National Congress of Italian Canadians. For Di Giovanni, this is a process that he defines, with a touch of enthusiasm, as "autonomous and irreversible, establishing at every level the self-realization of the community." Illustrating the community's accomplishments like Villa Colombo and Columbus Centre, Di Giovanni proceeds to examine the economic success and political ascent of Italian Canadians, as well as the role of the Catholic Church in the last quarter of the 20th century.

In the first 10 years of the present century the situation has changed fundamentally. Organizations such as the Congress and the Catholic Church have lost some of the influence they had in the past, for various reasons. The community is aging. The post-war immigrants are making room for the second and third generation, who are integrated and working within Canadian society, and no longer feel the need for community institutions. The children of the post-war immigrants are now well-established in local establishments, in various municipal councils, as well as federal and provincial governments, amply described by Di Giovanni.

Di Giovanni dedicates many pages to the inclusion of third language study in the regular elementary curriculum in Ontario. These programs surfaced after an epic struggle, and they distinguish Ontario because they have redefined the multicultural component and at the same time enrich the cultural life of the students. This is what signifies the Canadian mosaic.

This memoir by Alberto Di Giovanni is exuberant and optimistic, offering a detailed compendium of both the history of Canada and of the Italian Canadian community, and their mutual evolution. It is a satisfying panorama which, although the optimistic expressions reflect the author's nature, offers a picture of a community about which many have written, from interesting angles, but not always as comprehensive and complete as this one.

ODOARDO DI SANTO
Toronto, 2014

Introduction

"THE CHILDREN OF OUR CHILDREN, what will become of them? Who will they be? New ways will be discovered to find a place under the sun. And this will be achieved through war or by peaceful means? Or should we all move to Canada?" Words that seem to have been written in the present, but in reality they are the words of Hemingway and date back to 1926, the year he wrote "Banal Story," one of his *Forty-nine Stories*. When those words caught my eyes for the first time, I was 20 and I barely knew of the existence of Canada and of its endless landscape of snow, perched between the United States and the North Pole. That Hemingway could imagine that desert of snow as a destination for life unleashed a storm of questions. I found the first answers, which then generated more questions, along a sequence still now in progress. Then I found Canada, and I found Alberto Di Giovanni.

I am a man of the mountains, and so I know very well what real snow is, the kind that quietly, flake after flake, clothes the peaks and valleys with metres and metres in a dazzling mantle. That fascinating mantle, however, also knows how to be hostile if it envelopes you as it is taking shape. Every time that happened to me, seeing mounds of snow amplifying until they became insurmountable walls for the wheels on which my work depended, the saving illusion flashed before me of those superhuman locomotives of the Eurasian Orient Express or of the Canadian Royal Hudson, snorting billows of steam and piercing the night with their peremptory eyes, grinding thousands of kilometres

cutting through walls of snow with the ease of Moses engaged in opening the sea waves for his people.

It is precisely the image of a locomotive of the Royal Hudson committed to surmounting every obstacle interposed by the immensity of
Canada that comes to mind when you are present or a participant in the
aerobatic manoeuvres that Alberto Di Giovanni brings to the fulfilment
of his daring projects.

Canada's territory is the vastest on the planet, after that of Russia.
With its ten million square kilometres, it has an area equal to two and
a half times that of the 27 European Union member states. In so much
space, however, compared to the 460 million EU citizens, only 33 million people live in Canada.

One-third of the entire Canadian population is condensed in Ontario.
Toronto, which is the capital of Ontario, and the largest metropolis of
Canada, is home to 2.5 million people, of whom 700,000 are of Italian
ancestry. A beautiful and affable city (a far cry from the oppressive New
York), Toronto, for a sentimental man of Abruzzo which I long to be,
may seem like the hyperbolic fulfilment of a dream: less ancient than
L'Aquila and less of Abruzzese character than Pescara, it seems to be a
happy and successful blend between L'Aquila's ancient urban elegance
and Pescara's modern dynamism.

In Toronto, Bloor Street is the heart of city elegance. Along its golden
mile flow the super-sophisticated trendy streets of Yorkville. The win-
dows shine with the world's most famous designer labels and, like an
attraction at Disneyland, with which the architect Daniel Libeskind has
magnified the grand Royal Ontario Museum, there is an explosion of
polyhedra of glass and aluminium. But this is recent history. In past
times, Bloor was less trendy. A little more to the west of the Golden
Mile, Bloor intersects with Ossington Avenue. More than 30 years ago,
at Ossington, near the intersection with Bloor, there was (and I guess,
may still be), a former police station. Two floors with exterior façades
of brick painted a deep red tint, the window and door casings in a
sort of yellow-beige, with the fence of sturdy wire mesh enhanced by
generous splashes of a purple silver colour: a scene that could not be

more traditionally North American. Instead, in the "baccaiarda," that is in the back yard, an abrupt change of atmosphere: a group of seniors playing, without a shadow of a hurry, "bocce" or "tressette," a venerable jukebox offered a subdued background of mandolins and Mario-Merola. Inside the building, a further change of scene: the throngs of people, for the most part women, more or less young, all lustrous and yacking in English tinged with variegated Italian.

We were in the early eighties of the twentieth century. At that time, the magnificent Columbus Centre at the intersection of Dufferin and Lawrence was still under construction, while in the old police station, the major organizations of Italian Canadians found their headquarters, including the Centro Scuola e Cultura Italiana conceived by Alberto Di Giovanni. It is there that I met Alberto for the first time. Since then, many things have changed, a lot for the better and some for the worse, but Alberto is always the same, always the same irrepressible and genial locomotive that pulls everything and everyone every day to the most improbable stations invented by him and by himself set up along the less predictable paths of the human adventure.

The vital principle that moves and guides Alberto's daily life is supported by two fundamental pillars. The first emerges from one of the reasonings interwoven throughout the preface written by the same Alberto for *Dalla frontiera alle Little Italies* (From the border to the Little Italies), the book by Canadian historian Robert F. Harney which was published in Italy in 1984 in the series edited by Renzo De Felice for the publisher Bonacci:

> *In the years after World War II, Toronto, and other Canadian cities in general, have been the destination of Italian immigration more so than New York, Chicago, Sao Paulo or Buenos Aires. But in Italy, what Carlo Levi called the "American myth," has failed to adapt to this reality. Although thousands of Italian – above all in Abruzzo, Friuli, Lazio, Calabria and Sicily – have first-hand knowledge of the Italian-Canadian life, the idea that Italy has of America is often linked to images from the book of de Amicis,*

"Cuore," or to the Hollywood films. Whether at the popular or scientific level, little or nothing is known in Italy of the history and society of the Italian Canadians.

As for the second pillar, I borrow a few words written in the late 19th century by the distinguished economist Achille Loria, words which are still relevant today:

> *We Italians must intensely rejoice in the fact that imperialism,*
> *the morbus anglius par excellence, which, however, has spread all*
> *over the earth, and caused anguish in all nations, has not taken*
> *hold in our country perhaps for the very lively and incompressible*
> *spirit of freedom that characterizes our social life. And the impassioned hope that we hold for Italy is that it continue in this, its*
> *fecund way, and keep itself extraneous to the follies of colonialism*
> *and to imperialistic exploits that overwhelm all other states, and*
> *to focus all of its energies instead on intellectual imperialism, the*
> *only one a civil state should seek.*

I hope I have done justice to the brilliant Loria in my humble translation of his words.

And so, the daily life of Alberto follows this route, set down as the standard of living for himself and for the Centro Scuola: to allow, for the benefit of Canadian community, the expansion of influence of the Italian cultural heritage; to help develop in Italy the ability to understand authentic Italian Canadian reality. It is far from an easy undertaking, of which the modalities and the results Alberto narrates and records in this his stimulating book.

Moreover, it is his own family history which testifies to Alberto's unyielding dedication to the service of the two-way cultural link between Italy and Canada. While attending first year university in Toronto, Alberto made the acquaintance of one Caroline Morgan. A great attraction developed. Caroline helped to refine Alberto's English and Alberto helped Caroline to familiarize herself with Italian. After university, they lost sight of one another. But in fact, they had planned to meet again in Italy at some point of their trip, which each would make on their own, as a post-graduation vacation. They neglected, however, to establish an appointment. Instead, thanks to an incredible series of coincidences, they managed to find each other and meet in Florence. She was from Philadelphia and had gone to study in Toronto on the advice of her uncle, Msgr. J. Joseph Ryan, who was a prestigious scholar of the Middle Ages and taught courses at the University on canon law and medieval history. Once she graduated, Caroline went to Boston for her Master's degree, but ultimately chose to settle in Toronto. Her uncle's influence was the stimulant that allowed her to discover the world of Italian culture, of which she has become a serious connoisseur: when she married Alberto, in 1972 she also married Italian culture. A confirmed advocate of the necessity and, in fact, of the utility of multilingualism, she has never hesitated before the choice of Italian names for their children: Carlo Alberto (born November 1973), Franca (September 1977) and Annamaria (August 1982).

It is important to highlight a basic fact: for centuries, Canada has conformed to that orientation, not exclusively Canadian, known as "Anglo-conformity," whose ideology assumes that all immigrants must give up their own language and their own culture, to indulge in a full integration in the language and, of course, in the Anglo-Saxon culture. At some point, however, the strength of circumstances brought about that epochal change that has been the advent of the concept of "multicultural society." In assessable terms, the substantial transformation that occurred in the relations between ethnic groups within Canadian society was to be acknowledged: no longer dominant was the Anglo-Saxon faction. In fact, today, the 33 million citizens of Canada are only one-third of British origin; one-third are of French ancestry; and one third come from many other cultures, of which Italian is among the majority.

The structural change which Pierre Trudeau led to a legislative conclusion was launched in 1970 with the report of the government commission that, reaffirming "the principle of equality between the two founding peoples," that is, between the English and the French, introduced the recognition of the "contribution made from other ethnic groups to the cultural enrichment of Canada."

For a country where the English and the French are considered the founders and masters, and where Francophones have never resigned themselves to having succumbed to English speakers, while the latter have never forgiven the former's stubborn fidelity to their historical ancestry, the admission – legally sanctioned – not only of their existence but also of the importance of other cultures was a revolutionary event. However, between the affirmation of the principle and its realization, in refractory well-established reality, intervened years of obstacles, resistance, misunderstandings and boycotts. Therefore, one can easily imagine how difficult and magnificent was the work of Alberto and his partners and associates of the Centro Scuola, since at some point they, in helping to undermine centuries-old deposits of "Anglo-conformity," were the protagonists of that almost unbelievable result, thanks to which Italian in a few years has become "the largest source language taught in Ontario and across Canada," according to the authoritative statement of Arturo Tosi, coordinator in London of Bilingualism and Language Testing Project (see the Italian Overseas, Giunti, Florence 1991, p. 101).

The introduction of Italian courses in Canadian schools has become legend: Alberto narrates it with passion and accuracy in his book, framing it in an historical and analytical context that skilfully helps us understand all the cultural and social importance of that epochal time. In giving an account of the many other contributing undertakings of which he has been protagonist, Alberto also offers a valuable key that allows us to reach down to the core of the epic, outlining two illuminating stories: that of the formation of the Canadian nation, and that of the transformation of Italian immigrants from "Italians living in Canada" into "Italian Canadians," that is, "Canadians of Italian ancestry."

That first time at Ossington Avenue was for me revealing of many aspects of the professional competence and of the style of reasoning, earnestness and firmness of purpose with which Alberto was able to conceive and lead to fruition his cultural and social mission. In particular, as it happened, I mentioned something that I imagined to be unknown to him. I told him that, while he busied himself setting up Italian courses in Canadian schools, in Italy, a couple of years before, some sociologists had started to propagate the preposterous idea to supplant or, at most, juxtapose Italian with English. This issue had found for quite a while wide coverage in the press and not a few supporters, all of whom were out of breath with saying that, English being now the dominant language on the planet, young Italians who had not mastered English would all have remained unemployed. As I was telling him this, Alberto began rummaging through his files. Coming to sit by my side, he placed in front of me a cut-out from a major Canadian newspaper, the *Toronto Star*'s September 9, 1978 edition. That frippery of a proposal had ricocheted all the way there, and promptly found Alberto ready to show his stuff with a peppery and well-argued comment released to the newspaper:

> *There's no question of the importance of English in today's world. But it just can't replace Italian. That's nonsense. Italian students have every opportunity of learning English once they get to high school level. When parents request it, English is also taught at the elementary level. English is not a compulsory subject. But they have a choice, and English is one.*

Several years have passed. Alberto and I became friends and worked together on many beautiful things and perhaps even important ones. He has never changed, compared to what I knew of him from that first meeting: he is always attentive to the facts that move small as well as great things and involved in seeking out its causes, with the aim of engaging both thought and action in order to add a brick to the building of a better and more liveable world.

As for the bricks, over the years, the Columbus Centre has become one of the most fascinating places in the world among those created by the initiative of the Italian immigrants, and at one point, it made available within its space a more worthy home for the Centro Scuola. One evening, coming out of there, I took note for the first time of a curious coincidence: even the vast and inviting façades of the Columbus Centre are made of red brick, but, unlike the bland Anglo-Saxon style of "painted" red bricks of the old police station on Ossington Avenue, the bricks of the Columbus do not require periodic repainting, because we are dealing with those fine Italian exposed bricks that are intrinsically and indelibly red. A nice change of matter: from having to be content with "seeming" to actually "being."

ERRICO CENTOFANTI,
L'Aquila, 2014

ONE

Two Motherlands

ITALIAN EMIGRATION from the 19th to the 20th century is a grand and dramatic phenomenon of which its protagonist has been a throng estimated at 25 million people, which had as its goal nearly all the countries of northwestern Europe and the rest the world, and especially in North and South America and Australia. There are not many, in Italy as elsewhere, who have a real understanding of that phenomenon. In the imagination of those who have vague notions, there are two basic icons, almost always defined by an almost too persuasive myth: the Statue of Liberty, which greets and perhaps blesses the arrival in New York of the ships laden with aspiring immigrants; and Ellis Island, where the sorting and selection takes place for destinations in the Promised Land, and which often was also the antechamber of rejection for the unwelcome.

As for Canada, the arrival at harbour of migrants has had less romantic notions and what's more has been no less problematic, no less painful, no less humiliating. One arrived by ship to Halifax, and from there the journey continued towards Montreal or Toronto by train, in wagons used to carry livestock.

I was in some ways more privileged, having arrived in Toronto by plane, with a stop in Montreal. It was an evening at the beginning of April, 1963. I was 17 and I came from Roccamorice, an ancient hamlet clinging to the coastal mountains of Abruzzo. All I knew of the unknown country where I had landed was that my parents and some of my brothers were there, and that Canada was a boundless territory, which was said to be the "land of opportunity."

The new reality into which I had landed did not cause a traumatic impact; I did not arrive without points of reference, like most of those who had preceded me, and I did not experience the disorientation, so typical of immigrants. I, rather, was imbued with the feeling of having an exciting future before me, and I had the support of family, already settled for years in Toronto. For me, the yearning for the motherland was not an issue. In fact, I never had the time to succumb to that nostalgic longing, if not for a while, right in the beginning. Moreover, soon after the fifth year of residence in Canada I began to undertake the first of many frequent trips to Italy. Because of these I was able to keep alive that close relationship with the mother country that has characterized the entire course of my life. The first initiative was obviously that of socialization. The Italian community had been able to create various associations, including clubs and other types of organizations where both Italian and a wide range of regional dialects were spoken.

What appeared to me rather strange was my first contact with the Catholic Church. I came from a very different experience. In Italy there was large scale dissatisfaction with the customs and mentality considered of another era. We read challenging books from Catholic circles in France, dealing with the movement of the worker-priests. There emerged an exciting search for innovations, with a powerful thrust towards robust reform, so much so that the encyclical *Mater et Magistra* appeared to be a natural consequence, leading to the convening of the Second Vatican Council. In Canada, however, nothing of the sort was taking place; everything remained quiet and strictly traditionalist.

I joined the Young Christian Workers, an association whose corresponding body in Europe had developed a fervent and very effective movement in both social and cultural contexts. It was for me, however, a great disappointment. In Toronto, the only significant activity nurtured neither social change nor cultural ambitions of any kind, but rather simply facilitated the social encounter between boys and girls, not necessarily of Italian background, but definitely of Catholic faith. I turned away from the Young Christian Workers and began frequenting the Italo-Canadian Recreation Club on Brandon Avenue, the historic and popular home of Italians in Canada. This was chaired by John De Toro, a prominent and well liked figure in the community. De Toro was himself from Abruzzo (Fossacesia). He spoke rather poor Italian, but had a very good command of English. An unquestionably honest person, De Toro's reputation was considerable, both among the Anglo-Saxons, because of once having risked his life to save a police officer, and among the Italians, due to his irreproachable attitude towards his employees. It was he who presided over the committee created to raise funds in aid of Florence after the flood of 1966. In short, De Toro was the prominent exception of his social milieu, that of the "Notables," or people of power, generally coarse and arrogant, who for decades had exercised absolute authority over the Italian immigrants.

The ambience of the Italo-Canadian Recreation Club was basically of secular orientation and recreational character. We would meet for a chat, spend time playing a game of cards, and enjoy the evenings and weekend afternoons on the dance floor. At least here, however, we began to think more seriously about commitments towards cultural activities. And it was here that Bruno Mesaglio, a brilliant gentleman from Tuscany, created and astutely directed the Piccolo Teatro, an amateur theatre group that, notwithstanding its popular and traditional themes, however devoted to good taste, was able to promote in the community a love for Italian theatre. One sector of the Recreation Club was the Italo-Canadian Youth Club, which became an important gathering place for young people and an effective springboard for their active involvement in the community. Its president was Angelo Delfino, whose skilful and dynamic enthusiasm attracted a considerable number of young people. Here I was encouraged to initiate cultural activities, participate in debates, and contribute feature articles to a monthly magazine published by the club.

Early in 1966, I was able to recruit a group of young amateurs to mount a play, *I Benpensanti di Nicola Peccorelli*, which was performed on June 26 of that year. This was the beginning of my involvement with a series of productions that introduced me to Mesaglio's theatre, and resulted in an invitation to direct the Italian Club plays at St. Michael's College School. The youth section of the Italo-Canadian Recreation Club ended up slowly dying out, but it left in its place a valuable legacy, having helped to shape a generation of future entrepreneurs, directors and other key players in community life.

While still active in the Youth Club, I was invited to participate in a conference on human rights in Port Elgin, on Lake Huron. I was on a panel with a group of distinguished Canadians. To my surprise, my intervention made a big impression on the well-known journalist Scott Young, who commented on my contribution in his column in the *Globe and Mail*, August 25, 1966. With the encouragement of this experience, my focus matured and I decided to return to formal schooling. Shortly afterwards, in September, 1966, I applied for the so-called Western Year at St. Michael's College, University of Toronto.

Another organization, founded alongside the Italo-Canadian Recreation Club, had a considerable influence in promoting the Italian spirit within the Canadian context. It was the Toronto Italia Soccer Association, initially founded under the name of Italia Virtus, and chaired by Peter Bosa, who was subsequently appointed Senator by Prime Minister Trudeau. Even today, after more than half a century, there are those who longingly remember the early days of Canadian soccer at the Fred Hamilton and Stanley Parks. Those were years of great ardour and devotion among the Italian fans. The games became the moment when one could vent hidden feelings of nationalism. In fact, the names of the teams that competed were for the most part based on the various nations of origin. In 1962, Gino Ventresca, an Abruzzese from Sulmona, became president of Toronto Italia. A well-liked and respected figure in his community, Ventresca will later come to be recognized for the creation of Casa Abruzzo. Thanks to him, competitive Canadian soccer played among the various ethnic groups reached its peak. The matches were played at Varsity Stadium, which could accommodate more than 20,000 spectators.

This nationalistic spirit in sport was a preview of the outpouring which took place in July, 1982, when Italy won the World Cup of Soccer in Spain. Over 500,000 people flowed onto St. Clair Avenue West at Dufferin St. in a spontaneous celebration of pride in this victory. The Toronto media and general population were amazed at this unprecedented display, unmarred by any sign of violence, damage, or misbehaviour. Toronto would never be the same. Today, every four years during the World Cup competitions, crowds from every nation still gather at St. Clair and Dufferin to cheer and celebrate, without confrontation.

With the Italo-Canadian Youth Club behind me, and having now arrived at the University of Toronto, I joined its Italian Club, at the very time when it was the most active in the social and cultural life of the community. I was subsequently elected as its president just as a sense of renewal in '68 was beginning to take hold even among the Italian Canadians. The Italian Club had a long tradition of producing an annual play at Hart House Theatre, with a group of enthusiastic and talented young students. Some of the cast members included Guido Pugliese, who would later become a professor in the Italian department, and direct many plays himself. Also active in the productions were Susan Scotti, Maddeleine Manella, Teresa Patullo, Paolo Siraco, Gus Settecase, and the very talented Carmen Nepa and Mauro Cotechini. The general population of Italian speakers in Toronto attended these productions; they were not just for students. The Compagnia dei Giovani was subsequently formed out of the Italian Club, an amateur acting company that would make a considerable contribution to the Italian presence in Toronto's theatre scene.

During the same period there was also the decisive shift for the radical transformation of the Dante Alighieri Society from a dusty ivory tower for a few academics, which it had been until then, to a cauldron of cultural vitality still brilliantly effective in Toronto's intellectual arena. As part of the flourishing team that animated the Dante Alighieri

Society, it is important to remember the valuable work of Friulian Elio Costa, a professor of Italian literature, and Odoardo Di Santo, an Abruzzese from Rocca Pia, whom I had myself introduced to the community. Di Santo had arrived from Italy well equipped as a contributor to the Rome daily *La Giustizia* and would soon undertake his brilliant career in journalism and to the important roles he would fill as a parliamentarian within the New Democratic Party.

A decisive share of the success of the activities of the renewed Dante Alighieri Society must be attributed to Fabio Rizi, a truly admirable person. I remember Fabio, an Abruzzese from Corfinio, as a broad-minded, serious and hardworking gentleman who never involved himself in the controversial skirmishes that unfortunately have long plagued the associations of Italian Canadians. Rizi was the facilitator of the St. Clair Public Library at Dufferin, which he placed at our disposal, allowing it to become the hub of cultural activities of the Dante Society. In those years, the Italian Cultural Institute had not yet been created nor did the Columbus Centre yet exist. We would meet in Rizi's library where well-attended presentations of all kinds would take place. It was there that we were to host, among the many other illustrious visitors from Italy, Giorgio Bassani and even Umberto Eco. Likewise, there were poetry readings with a young Pier Giorgio Di Cicco, later the Poet Laureate of Toronto, and Len Gasparini, poet and short story writer.

Thus far I've moved rather quickly with respect to recalling my early days in Canada, but it now seems appropriate to return there for a while. My first contact with the country that would become my second home was not necessarily the often painful experience endured by many others. Unlike so many migrants, who began with the hope of getting a few years of hard work abroad and eventually returning enriched to their homeland, I was not in a hurry, nor even wished to return home. I was thirsty for knowledge and the horizons that Canada was revealing to my imagination. I could not have dreamt of living in the beautiful but poor mountain regions of Abruzzo back then. From the beginning, I was aware that I would have two homelands: that of my roots and that of my growth, the one and the other inextricably fused in my heart and in my mind.

The time of my arrival in Toronto was a period of transition in the evolution of the Canadian nation. I was dropping anchor in an English-speaking country, which was close-minded and harboured lingering bigotry. They called us "wop," an obviously pejorative racial slur which implied "losers," it being defined in the Oxford dictionary "to whop," or "defeat." It was Prime Minister Lester B. Pearson who led the retreat from this backward phase.

The first two most important things for me became the need to work and the need to learn English. Without either of these, I would not be able to continue my studies at the university, which was my prime objective. The first job I held was as a dishwasher at Mario's Spaghetti House. I was making a career out of this, especially because I was able to learn English quickly; soon, I was promoted to waiter. Mario's Spaghetti House became my "Statue of Liberty," where I had been welcomed and where Toronto was giving me its blessing. The Spaghetti House provided work and promising prospects.

In the factories and in construction work there were many problems, both because of the difficulty of the language and for the hardship of the hierarchical rapport. Whatever their country of origin, however, there also existed much solidarity among immigrants. When I took the opportunity for employment in a bank, I experienced the obvious and often oppressive and intolerant attitude of the haughty "wasp," the "White Anglo-Saxon Protestant," who regarded themselves as the city's natural leaders. At that point, I was gripped by a strong desire to attend university, which would mean not only access to an intellectual formation par excellence but also to a mastery of the language and a discernible ease such as to remove any feelings or sense of insecurity. I had finally achieved familiarity with English, enough to afford me the long-coveted enrolment at university. I left the bank with many asking me: "Are you crazy? You have an important job and you leave it behind? When will you be able to find better?"

At St. Michael's College, the Catholic college of the University of Toronto, I found my niche despite the initial difficulties caused by my English, still somewhat weak and conventional. I found there, in fact, a marked difference in attitudes with respect to the outside world. Friendly relations were formed among students and teaching staff; a deliberate atmosphere of hard work permeated throughout. It left no room for slackers (whether they be students or teachers) and did not get hung up on bureaucratic complications. Among the teachers who, for their preparation and seriousness, have had a strong influence on my education, I must recognize the palaeographer Fr. Leonard Boyle, O.P. of the Pontifical Institute of Medieval Studies, who later became Prefect of the Vatican Library; and Father Robert Madden, member of the Congregation of St. Basil and Professor of English Literature, who devoted great time and attention to me because, as he said, he saw my significant potential.

The Congregation of St. Basil, known as the Basilians, enjoyed great prestige in the educational arena in North America. These were the years of student protest and the Order reacted by initiating an intense rapport of dialogue between teachers and pupils from which evolved what has been defined as "the community of scholars." Unfortunately, the Order headed towards declining numbers in the 1980's. I feel nostalgia for that kind of education, aimed at the student's growth as a whole and not conditioned merely by seeking economic advantages. To be able to finance my studies, during the summer months I busied myself working at the headquarters of a political party, as a union organizer, as a reporter and later as a consultant for COSTI.

Following a hard-won campaign, I was voted in as member of the Student Council of the University of Toronto with an unpredictable harvest of votes, despite my strongly accented English. In those years, I met and befriended several outstanding students, including Mark Freiman, later an influential lawyer; Jeff Rose, who would become the leader of CUPE; Michael Ignatieff, author and intellectual; and Bob Rae, who would be recognized as a Rhodes Scholar, the most prestigious scholarship of the English-speaking world. Rae would later become the

Premier of Ontario and subsequently the Interim Leader of the Federal Liberal Party in Ottawa. When he became Premier he was a member of the New Democratic Party, the first in Ontario to win a majority under the banner of that party. His was an experience of high-profile government, although in many respects unfortunate, coinciding as it did with a period of economic recession rooted in the global economy of the time.

Rae was one of the most qualified of Canadian politicians; there existed a cultural gap between himself and all the others. Giulio Andreotti, who was very well informed and perceptive in judging characters and situations, said after a meeting with Rae that he was "the best after Trudeau." Rae had requested that I act as interpreter at that meeting, but my work would be very slight, as the two quickly realized that they understood one another conversing in French. My friendship with Rae has been a constant in my life as he has on his part always held our rapport in high regard, so much so that, on the occasion of a visit to Italy, he asked me to accompany him to my town of Roccamorice and L'Aquila.

While in university and right after graduation, I participated on several different community undertakings. In April, 1970, I was elected a member of the first Board of Directors of the newly formed FACI (Federation of Italian Associations of Canada); towards the end of 1972 I became a consultant in the direction of the Humber York Centre, an outreach body from Humber College created to help identify the educational needs of the citizens of the area, and develop new programs. In April, 1974, I was elected Vice President of the Dante Alighieri Society of Toronto, of which I later became President. I then took the helm of the Multicultural Theatre Association, and of various other initiatives emerging in the Italian community. I was one of the founders of the National Congress of Italian-Canadians, entering the National Council in March, 1974, then becoming National Secretary in November, 1982. I was always very active and dynamic and soon realized that I was usually the youngest among my peers.

Throughout my university years, the difficulties and insecurities had begun to slowly fade, taken over by a more easy-going and pleasant adjustment. After obtaining my degree in Italian Language and Literature, I gave myself to teaching for a few years at St. Michael's College School and at Humber College. Then in 1976, I took the initiative of creating the Centro Scuola e Cultura Italiana, putting all my energy, knowledge, and passion into this new reality. I probably could not have conceived the idea of the Centro Scuola, much less bring it to fruition, without the concurrence of two fundamental circumstances: one due to the cultural revolution of the seventies which radically changed Canadian politics; and the other which resulted from my continued interest and contact with the academic world.

In those years, the shining star of Pierre Trudeau, Prime Minister from 1968-1979 and again from 1980-84, was particularly auspicious. Canada was crossing a euphoric modernizing path triggered and fuelled by the courageous and farsighted initiatives of a bright and charming Prime Minister, a period now known as "Trudeaumania." The politics of multiculturalism led by Trudeau became the beating heart of Canada, a country that finally took flight towards a role of international excellence. For Italian-Canadians that was a magical time, thanks to which it would be possible to achieve both political and social positions hitherto unthinkable. Magnificent! Moreover, economic conditions improved visibly. However, it is my view that that special moment also held the germ of a terrible risk, had Italian Canadians continued to allow themselves to become melded into the Anglo-Saxon cauldron as they had for decades practically been forced to do. The opportunity of multiculturalism had to be exploited wisely in the early stages, in order to be able to create adequate instruments that would protect and enhance the heritage of both the Italian language and identity in the context of full membership in the new Canadian homeland.

Having conceived both the needs and the aims, those instruments needed to be created. At this point, another fundamental circumstance evolved within the university setting. My studies with Robert F. Harney, my history teacher, had been instrumental towards my academic development. Harney had specialized at the University of California, Berkeley, with a dissertation on the Risorgimento and then accepted a professorship at the University of Toronto. His many-faceted interests were dedicated primarily to the phenomenon then virtually ignored in the academic world: immigration. A strong affinity grew between us, at first formed of mutual esteem and then also through collaboration.

So it was in the university years that I began to conceive a project that, in the context of the new multicultural politics of Canada, aimed at enhancing the cultural heritage of immigrants. The aim was to stir pride in one's mother tongue and at the same time to induce the institutions to introduce those languages within the educational curriculum. That became the core concept of the Heritage Languages Program and, at the same time, the Centro Scuola. In organizing that project I had the support of two key stakeholders: Father Nicola De Angelis, a priest of extraordinary intellectual stature who in later years was to receive distinction as bishop; and Professor Julius Molinaro, a member of the Royal Society of Canada, which is the equivalent of Italy's Accademia dei Lincei. In the early post-war years Professor Molinaro founded the University Student Club and re-founded in 1956 the Dante Alighieri Society, which had been dissolved when it had become a tool of fascist propaganda. He was also the first President of the Association of Italian Studies.

Another prominent personality who was of great support to me was Gianrenzo Clivio, a young professor of Italian at the University of Toronto, noted scholar of linguistics from the University of Turin, and then from Harvard University. Although he had arrived in North America only a few years before, he realized immediately the need for the Italian community in Canada to act independently with respect to the diplomatic authorities.

The philosophy of the Centro Scuola is to act locally and autonomously, and this belief has prevailed thanks to the contributions and vision of other community leaders, such as Celestino De Iulis, in the area of culture; Sam Marafioti, one of the elected Trustees of the Catholic School Board of Toronto; and Tony Silipo, Chairman of the Toronto School Board, the only Italian Canadian to ever be so. In later years, he would also become Minister of Education. Based on the shared belief that Italian culture constitutes a heritage for all humanity and not just for the descendants of Italian immigrants, I also had the great privilege of the cooperation of the renowned scholar Fr. Leonard Boyle, mentioned above. Another ally was Mark Freiman, a university teacher and later a renowned lawyer. The support of the National Congress of Italian Canadians was also of paramount importance. It was then presided over by Laureano Leone, who would later become a member of the Legislature of Ontario.

I can say that I have done my utmost, and then some, in the years that have witnessed Italian Canadians acquiring the full status of citizenship and nationality, without the slightest damage to the proud claim of our Italian roots. Italians have won through hard work, intelligence and honesty the right to feel and be accepted as authentic citizens of Canada. But the path was neither short nor smooth, nor could it be understood in all its complexity without reflecting on the whys and the wherefores of what Canada has been in the past and what it has become today. One must acknowledge the price paid by Italian Canadians for our achievements, in terms of the difficulty, the anxiety, the anguish and the moral and material sacrifices, in the context in which we found ourselves living and working. This was once a country which had not yet arrived at defining a national identity; a country torn from an old and sometimes brutal conflict between its two major components of language and culture; in doubt as to the kinds of relationship it had with the mass of immigrants belonging to dozens of different cultures; a country pervaded by recurrent uncertainties about its economic and social structure and about its place in the international scene.

In the following chapters I endeavour to provide a comprehensive picture for those who have little experience with the reality of Italian immigration to Canada. I hope to absolve, albeit minimally, the huge debt of gratitude that I have accrued towards my two homelands, equally loved and honoured by me.

TWO

The Canadian Mosaic

I⊤ IS AN AGE-OLD DILEMMA, attempting to create a true Canadian nation whose most critical issue over the past two centuries has unfolded around the conflict between two main linguistic-cultural elements: Anglophone and Francophone. Everything begins in 1763 when, after the Seven Years' War on North American soil, Britain prevailed over France.

In 1534 Jacques Cartier raised the French flag as a first step towards the future Canada. Nouvelle France was beginning to take shape. That moment signalled the decline of the dominion of the Inuit and other aboriginal nations, descendants of the Indo-Europeans who had arrived there 40,000 years before through the Bering Strait. Around the year 1000 the Vikings had not been able to maintain their occupation against the endurance of the natives. The explorations of John and Sebastian Caboto from the late 15th to the early 16th century gave substance to a colonial organization in constant growth as far as territorial extension and production of wealth. The unbridled power of the French located to the north of the American colonies of Great Britain was felt in London as a potential threat to their interests. According to the practice of the time, this could not but be followed by a push toward war. And so, after nearly a quarter of a millennium, New France came under British rule, well before the American colonies to the south fought to gain independence, and proclaim themselves the United States of America.

Waves of British immigration followed. The initial one was required in order to create a balance with respect to the legacy of French-speaking New France. The one that followed, in 1781, was a result of the need to welcome the diehard loyalists who refused to remain in the former colonies now recognized as the United States of America. Finally, the massive influx of the British and Irish came from the motherland to find new lives in the new land. This latter swell had been deemed necessary in order to strengthen the defence capabilities of the colony, in view of a possible new threat of invasion by the U.S. after the blunt attempt with the war of 1812-14. A further flood of tens of thousands of English speaking immigrants took place following the devastating famine that struck Ireland in 1846.

The Francophone presence, beginning with the 16th century, was centred primarily in today's Quebec. Anglophones, meanwhile, began to colonize Ontario, which until that time had been almost entirely uninhabited. With the British North America Act in 1867, the British Parliament, in declaring the unification of New Brunswick and Nova Scotia to what had been Nouvelle France, created "a single domain under the name of Canada." That point forever established the incontestable Anglophone hegemony in the largest territory in the world after the Russian Federation.

However, after two and a half centuries, the descendants of the original French colonists had acquired the mentality of "inhabitants" and, having suffered the termination of the political connection with France because of the British conquest, they perceived themselves essentially as a subjugated people. On the other hand, Anglophones remained in effect British citizens and saw themselves as the conquerors, as well as harbingers of a superior society. In short, the Canadian nation did not exist independently, nor did it possess a concrete reason for being. The Aboriginal component was confined to irrelevant marginalization, the underlying issue being the uncompromising opposition between imperial nationalism of the Anglo-Canadians and the Canada-centric nationalism of the French Canadians. Not even the persistent shadow of annexation by the United States could put in motion a merging of purpose able to create the nation that was for many, however, a fervent aspiration.

Events progressed very slowly, chiefly because of the long process of evolution that has characterized the history of the British colonial empire, from its beginnings in the 17th century right up to the first half of the 20th. The last decades of the 19th century saw the start in the colonial territories of the first communities to be self-governed, or "dominions," whose significant contribution in committing to the British in the Great War would then bring about their own emancipation.

With the British North America Act of 1867, the British Parliament created the Canadian statehood (though always under the colonial rule), and above all provided the basic nucleus of a future national identity: its name. Possible names such as Victorialand, Boreal, Cabotia, Tuponia, Norland, Hochelaga were wisely discarded, choosing instead the word "Canada" which in the Iroquoian language means "community." The British North America Act contained what in fact is the first Constitution of Canada, which stated, among other things, that governments elected by the people would be the most important institutions of the country. However, the Constitution founded a state with limited sovereignty, since it did not come from the will of the Canadian people but was the result of a "concession" made by the British Parliament.

Twenty years later came the first authoritative expression of a national identity capable of moving everyone deeply:

> We are Canadians. Below the island of Montreal the water that
> comes from the north from the Ottawa unites with the waters
> that come from the western lakes. But uniting they do not mix.
> There they run parallel, separate, distinguishable, and yet are one
> stream, flowing within the same banks, the mighty St. Lawrence,
> and rolling on toward the sea. This is a perfect image of our
> nation."

These are words that Wilfrid Laurier, long before becoming Prime Minister of Canada, delivered in Toronto during his memorable speech of December 10, 1886. On another occasion, Laurier similarly expressed another effective image of Canada that he hoped to see flourish:

> *When in England, I visited one of these models of Gothic architecture, which the hand of genius, guided by an unerring faith, had moulded into an harmonious whole. This cathedral was made of granite, oak and marble. It is the image of the nation I wish to see Canada become. For here, I want the granite to remain the granite, the oak to remain the oak, the marble to remain the marble. Out of these elements I would build a nation great among the nations of the world.*

In this sort of a daydream of Laurier's, one can anticipate that concept which postulates the Canadian nation as a "mosaic" of different nationalities, a concept which will later be widely asserted, argued and somehow practiced during the 20th century. However, despite the willingness of Laurier, the inter-cultural conflict appeared far from being overcome. Most of the English-speaking Protestants had in mind just that, a strictly English-speaking Protestant Canada. By contrast, the Francophones, almost all Catholics, and with the support of a significant minority of Anglophones, cultivated the dream of a bilingual and bicultural Canada.

Between 1896 and 1911, the action of Laurier, the first Francophone to lead a federal government, was of exceptional importance, in order to create both a climate of moderation and constructiveness in the domestic confrontation, as well as to safeguard the principles that would guarantee the attainment of independence from the British imperial system for a future, more united and stronger, Canadian entity. The age-old issues of "separate schools," that is, educational institutions reserved for the Catholics in Ontario and Protestants in Quebec, and the formalizing of bilingualism found satisfactory resolution in much of the country. This

occurred at the same time as the implementation of a massive program of infrastructure and industrial development which removed
many of the reasons for social disadvantage underlying the ethno-
cultural conflict. On the international front, Laurier, despite the
highly contested military support given to Britain's war against the
Boers in South Africa, maintained a steadfast distance from sub-
mission to the basic principle of British imperialism. In London,
on March 13 , 1903, in the House of Commons, he declared: "*The
British Empire is composed of a galaxy of free nations all owing the
same allegiance to the same sovereign, but all owing paramount allegiance to their respective peoples.*"

A burst of fierce opposition infighting occurred in 1917, in reaction to obligatory conscription decreed to strengthen the Canadian
intervention in the Great War going on in Europe: mutual accusations of betrayal of tradition and of the national interest raged at
length between the Anglophones and the Francophones.

Beginning in the 1920s, England commenced the informal use
of the name of the British Commonwealth of Nations to designate
a "group of nations with self-government" within the empire; the
intent of which was to highlight the unity of an articulated body in
the autonomous communities, none subordinate to the other, united
by a common bond of allegiance to the Crown, and all contestants
in the pursuit of the shared "common good." In the political language of English dating from the time of Cromwell, and because of
its literal meaning of "common good," the word "commonwealth"
is equivalent to the concept of "res publica," of which the notion
of "republic" is drawn from Roman Law. The expression "British
Commonwealth of Nations" and its political-administrative meaning became official with the Statute of Westminster of 1931; that is,
with the approval of the Parliament of the United Kingdom of Great
Britain which recognized, among other things, full legislative autonomy for the dominions. The path of the Canadian State towards
full independence from Britain proceeded thus, albeit slowly. The
Canadian nation, however, still remained a muddle. Its potential for

consolidation still remained highly problematic, above all because of the unresolved conflict between Anglophones and Francophones.

A decisive contribution to the launching of that turning point came in 1938 with the appearance of the *Canadian Mosaic*, a book that had wide resonance and which finally opened a new and constructive trend of thought. The author was John Murray Gibbon, a writer of wide interests, of diverse international experience, broad-minded, and possessing a unique quality; that of being himself an immigrant. Born in 1875 in Sri Lanka, the country once known as Ceylon, he received his education at the University of Aberdeen, Oxford and Göttingen, and at 38 years of age had arrived in Canada.

A quarter-century of immersion in Canadian daily life and of reflections on the characteristics and problems of that kaleidoscopic reality led Gibbon to develop the all-new theory of a national mosaic in which each language group maintains its own distinct identity, yet contributes to making the nation a single entity. Presented so sparingly, Gibbon's theory may seem trivial, if not, with the hindsight of today, stating the obvious. But in the 1930s, it was revolutionary. No one had ever before conceived the idea that a nation could be the result of several diverse entities, cooperating with dignity and without any one dominant component. This idea was all the more radical considering that the dominant theory at the time had been borrowed from the powerful neighbouring United States of America: the Melting Pot, that is, the crucible in which all immigrants had to get approval from the dominant Anglo-Saxon component. Replacing the "melting pot" with the "mosaic" became the guiding principle for the development of a different interpretation of immigration and for the establishment of an innovative national policy. However, the new intellectual ferment and the overall review of political stereotypes would not have been sufficient to regenerate the old dream of a precise Canadian national identity, if at the same time there hadn't intervened changes, no less drastic, in the international context.

After the Second World War, Britain had to gradually give up its imperialist notion towards relations with the colonies. First, the adjective *British* disappears, updating the name of that sort of federation of dominions to *The Commonwealth of Nations*; then the word *dominion* is replaced by the phrase *Member of the Commonwealth*. Clearly, what was at hand were not only changes in terminology, but significant transformations: relations between Britain and the former colonies now appeared increasingly to be cast in economic and cultural terms and less and less as political subjection. However, there was still a long way to go before the multicultural Canada theorized by Gibbon became a political process finally transforming Canada into a "Nation" rather than simply a "state."

The signs of the true nature of multiculturalism began tentatively to appear in legislation with the Canadian Declaration of Human Rights, adopted by the Federal Government in 1960. This, however, remained for more than 20 years simply an admonition against discrimination, with no significant impact on jurisdiction.

Gibbon died in 1952, but the echo of his *Canadian Mosaic*, though far from extinct, necessitated some effective renewal. The renewal came in 1963, once again as a result of a book, although, this time, not a Canadian one. To strengthen the scientific background of multiculturalism, which had not yet taken off, was *Beyond the Melting Pot*, a book which proposed a thorough study of the role of ethnic components in the political, economic and cultural life of New York. The authors, Glazer and Moynihan, who in later years would become a distinguished professor of Harvard University and a prominent member of the Senate respectively, had prepared the study through the analysis of the five major ethnic groups of New York: African-Americans, Puerto Ricans, Jews, Italians and Irish. In a review of nearly 20 years later (Current Contents, January 7, 1980), Glazer points out that the study of the five groups was based on the history and the economic role of each group, and "what emerged from these orientations as somewhat original was the idea of the ethnic group not only surviving from the age of mass immigration, but (becoming) something of a new creation, and thus we could not expect rapid assimilation but an extended persistence, even as each group underwent change."

Nowadays, *Beyond the Melting Pot* is a classic, but its appearance in the United States sparked surprise and dismay, both in academic circles, which remained still far from approaching issues of immigration, and within the general public. The Canadian reception was much more attentive, of course, already having been sensitised by Gibbon's rationale and its further development. In an interview with Jane Perlez published on December 3, 1983, in the *New York Times*, Moynihan notes that the book's claims had received resounding proof, time and time again, for having hit the mark. For example, in the census of 1980 in Tennessee, "People there still think of themselves as English, Irish or Scottish, and they've been in those hills for centuries." At the national level, that same census, which for the first time asked to indicate ancestral origins, pointed out that 83% of respondents declined membership in at least one ethnic group while only 6% considered themselves "American," period. The comparison with the results of the Canadian national census of 2006 which amounted respectively to 80% and 5% is startling.

In 1963, the same year that *Beyond the Melting Pot* was released, Lester Pearson became the Prime Minister, and led Canada until 1968, when Pierre Trudeau would succeed him. The 20 years 1963-84, marked by the governments of Pearson and Trudeau, were the culminating point of the long, arduous road towards the conquest of Canada's national identity and independence. Pearson arrived at the helm of the government backed by an extraordinary curriculum: history professor and coach for ice hockey at the University of Toronto, not to mention, a high-profile diplomat, Foreign Minister, protagonist in the founding process of the UN, creator of the Emergency Force of the United Nations for peace-keeping missions, staunch broker of the 1956 resolution to the explosive Suez crisis and thus, awarded the Nobel Peace Prize. His minority Liberal Government, with the support of the social-democratic New Democratic Party, created, through Medicare, the first public health care system of the American continent. He introduced the Federal retirement plan and the Student Loan program; enacted legislation for limiting the work week to 40 hours; established a minimum wage, and a two week vacation leave; constituted fundamental measures to ensure women equal rights, and initiated reforms that brought levels of unemployment to an all-time low; he abolished restrictions to immigration of the non-white, and maintained firm resistance to pressure from the States for intervention in the Viet Nam war.

Pearson's thrust towards the creation of modern Canada was not only felt in the area of economy and social affairs, but was also a powerful influence on the affirmation of national identity and on the preparation for independence. While only symbolic gestures, his actions would have a decisive impact which would be both emotional and distinguishing. For example, he insisted that he no longer wished to be identified as an Anglo-Saxon but as a Canadian, and he oversaw the replacement of the British flag with a new national flag, red and white, and dominated by the maple leaf, which was adopted on February 15, 1965, after decades of controversy, and even bitter opposition.

In addition, Pearson laid out the conditions so that, not much later, French also would become the official language alongside English, while at the same time, resolutely weakening the secessionist ambitions of the French, who had hoped for the onset of influential international support after the disruptive speech of "Vive le Québec libre!" delivered in Montreal in 1967 by the French President, Charles de Gaulle. No less important was a parliamentary speech delivered in 1966. On that occasion, Pearson coined the neologism "patriation," a concept which would influence the outcome of the fervent debate on the Constitution, after many decades.

"We intend to do everything we can to have repatriated the Constitution of Canada," said Pearson. With that, he cleared the path of all the complicated hypotheses in drafting a new text, and opened the way for a procedure which would be neither simple nor sweeping, but could be realistically pursued with success. The legislation then in place had been passed by the British Parliament in 1867, a law that only the latter would have been able to modify. While in accordance

with the principles of full national sovereignty, the Constitution could now be amended only by the Canadian Parliament without any British interference. "Patriation" meant: "Let us repatriate the Constitution as it is and put off to more peaceful times the introduction of any changes that may be deemed necessary, and to which we Canadians alone will proceed without having to seek the approval of others." In fact, it was in this way that, albeit with more red tape and no less minor conflict, national sovereignty was finally won.

THREE

Towards a New Canadian Identity

1967 IS A PIVOTAL YEAR: it is the celebration of the Canadian Centennial, the centenary of the Confederation of Canadian States created by the British Parliament with the British North America Act of 1867. Lester Pearson announces his decision to leave, in the short term, the leadership of the country. By inviting Pierre Trudeau to take over the Ministry of Justice, he basically made the move to appoint his successor. Pierre Elliott Trudeau was born in Montreal to French- and English-speaking parents, and he firmly opposed Quebec's separatist claims. He was a passionate interpreter of a future social vision, and an ingenious composer of bold political plans with, among other things, the repeal of the criminal code laws against homosexuality and the legalization of divorce, to justify his slogan: "There is no place for the state in the bedrooms of the nation." With all this, Trudeau won the overwhelming support of young people and great thinkers, so that in April, 1968, they helped him secure the leadership of the Liberal Party, the main political force in the country, and subsequently, his appointment as Prime Minister.

The year 1967 was one of exhilarating euphoria, dominated by great structural achievements, and economic and social issues that over the past century had raised Canada from the condition of a

territory subject to colonial exploitation to a flourishing and innovative industrial power. Among the events of that memorable year,
the most distinct was Expo 67, which presented in the spectacular
pavilions of Montreal, exhibits of the best of Canada's creativity and
of many other countries for the world to admire. Soon afterwards,
however, much of the elation for the goals that had been achieved
began to dissipate over the course of a decade filled with considerable difficulties, jarring anxiety and exhausting debates on how to
escape from the growing web of distress. And it kept mounting: a
pounding inflation, the rising public debt, the shocking effects of
the global oil crisis, a harsh economic recession and the disturbing
resurgence of the Quebec separatist movement.

Thirty years later, the journalist and historian Pierre Berton would
publish a book to argue that 1967 had been *The Last Good Year*.
Even if unrealistic, this statement provides a picture of the moral
climate that took hold after the Canadian Centennial. It was above
all the uneasiness on account of the Francophones, even more than
any financial and economic turmoil, that deflated Canadian morale
after the "Last Good Year." In reality, in the rest of the federation and
in significant niches in the very same Quebec, most of the age old
ancestral intolerance towards Anglophones was now water under
the bridge. This was especially the case among the youth and the
more educated. However, in Quebec, unyielding separatist hardlin-
ers constituted anything but irrelevant fringe groups. The displeas-
ure of the French did not derive only from the war lost a long time
before against the British army, or from any linguistic discrimination
or from the limited power accorded to the French in the decision-
making structures of the federal government. Rather, the resentment
was actively and robustly fed by both an economic and cultural
inadequacy.

Since 1875, education and health in Quebec were firmly in the
hands of the Catholic Church, which had obtained the monopoly
from the provincial government and which excluded any interference on the part of the latter. The poor quality of basic training and

24

the high cost of higher education ensured access to university studies only for a small elite group, while health services run as charities
kept the bulk of the population in rather precarious condition. Even
after the Second World War, unlike the rest of the country, things
had not changed: the conservative politics of the provincial government and the frailness of cultural and health issues for the population denied Quebec any modernization and economic development.
Then, in the 1960s, this situation underwent a sudden stimulation
as a result of the so-called Quiet Revolution. Massive investments
were made in the infrastructure and services to citizens; the production and distribution of electricity were nationalized, and incisive
social reforms were made. The most meaningful of the revolutionary changes was the rapid process of secularization of society and
the consequent public administration and management of education
and health. Indeed, the success of the Quiet Revolution allowed society to make progress, but economic and social growth, on the other
hand, had a disturbing impact, inciting those groups of unyielding
nationalists to claim political independence with unusual vehe-
mence from a predominantly Anglophone federal government. The
encouragement which came in 1967 from the irresponsible "Vive le
Québec libre!" of Charles de Gaulle, stoked the fire which ushered
in the violence: terrorist attacks, kidnappings of well-known figures,
and the assassination in 1970 of the Deputy Prime Minister, Pierre
Laporte. The toughness and the ability of Pierre Trudeau, and the
strength of democratic institutions, were able to defuse the resulting instability such that in the Olympic Games of Montreal in 1976,
one might easily recognize the symbolic culmination of one of the
most dramatic decades of Canadian history. The "Quebec question,"
in any case, still remains in the background of national issues, even
if no longer associated with violence, nor with separatist ambitions.
After failed attempts in 1980 and in 1995, Quebec chose the path of
the referendum to attain sovereignty.

A major initiative to pave the way towards overcoming
Francophone animosity, as well as the problems associated with the

intricate multi-ethnicity of the country, was launched in July 1963 by the Pearson government through the establishment of the Royal Commission on Bilingualism and Biculturalism. The Commission was given a mandate both very complex and delicate:

> To inquire into and report upon the existing state of bilingualism
> and biculturalism in Canada and to recommend what steps should
> be taken to develop the Canadian Confederation on the basis of
> an equal partnership between the two founding races, taking into
> account the contribution made by the other ethnic groups to the
> cultural enrichment of Canada and the measures that should be
> taken to safeguard that contribution.

The work of the Royal Commission on Bilingualism and Biculturalism would continue for several years and its results would have a decisive influence on the extensive action led by Pierre Trudeau. Moreover, without the measures of the Pearson government, the work brilliantly carried out by Trudeau would not have been possible. One must not overlook the influence exercised on the formation of the guidelines of the political forces and on general public opinion by the appearance in 1965 of the book *The Vertical Mosaic* by the sociologist, John Arthur Porter. Taking the idea developed in 1938 by John Murray Gibbon, that of "a nation made up of a mosaic of different language groups," Porter analysed the Canadian situation with two innovative points of view: the decision-making mechanisms of the political and economic bodies, and the inequality of opportunities offered to the individual. Having established that "*individuals or groups at the top of our institutions can be designated as elites*," Porter argues that "*elites both compete and co-operate with one another: they compete to share in the making of decisions of major importance for the society, and they co-operate because together they keep the society working as a going concern.*" Consequently, the society that Gibbon saw as an "ethnic mosaic" for Porter was, yes a "mosaic," but a vertical one, namely, cultural. It was precisely the expression "cultural mosaic" that took hold in the development of the emerging new Canada, thus providing the views from which would come the politics of "multiculturalism." At that point, it became inevitable, as much as crucial, to ask oneself: "We Canadians, who are we? Where do we wish to go?"

The concept of the national community revolved around the *Two Fundamentals*, i.e., Anglo-Saxon and French. And yet, what of the others? What of the Germans and Italians, the two major components, after the predominant ones? And what about the rest, starting with the Aboriginals right up to the more than 200 minor groups? In the Ontario Legislature, Odoardo Di Santo put the matter in terms that made an impact, wondering if the non-Anglo-Saxon and non-Francophone should be considered as "Incidentals," that is, as irrelevant accessories of the nation. It is finally during the years of Trudeau as Prime Minister that we gain a glimpse of the new Canadian identity, no longer based on the *Two Fundamentals* but rather on the "fundamental of the whole" of its multiple components.

FOUR

Trudeau and Multiculturalism

THE ROYAL COMMISSION on Bilingualism and Biculturalism, with its two reports published respectively in 1965 and 1969, recommended the introduction of radical reforms, among which were those aimed at correcting the inadequacy of the French presence in the decision-making bodies of the country, and those based on the recognition of both the needs and the contributions made to the nation by the other ethnic groups. The conclusions of the Commission, supported by the Liberal Party, the Progressive Conservative Party and the New Democratic Party, despite the strenuous filibuster of conservative forces, gave wings to the policy pursued by Trudeau. It was in the years of the Trudeau government, from 1968-1984, with a short break of a Conservative government between 1979 and 1980, that the policy of creating a "just society" was pursued, in which every citizen would "be Canadian" without linguistic, ethnic, sexual, or economic discrimination, and each individual could avail himself or herself of the same opportunities.

With the Official Languages Act of 1969, bilingualism was introduced, resulting in a wide-ranging reform of the education system and compelling the Federal public service to use simultaneously both English and French in official acts and both languages in communicating with citizens.

With the intent of extinguishing the old conflicts and enhancing the prospects offered by the influx of immigrants, the Multiculturalism Act of 1971finally surpassed the logic of the "three solitudes," that is, of the historic isolation of one from the other of the Anglophone, Francophone and Aboriginal units, and ushered in that multicultural reality that recognizes in all Canadians the right to maintain one's own traditions, the free profession of one's own religion, and access to schooling in one's own language of origin.

Then came the radical reform of immigration policy, with the Immigration Act of 1976, the substance of which was "to support the attainment of longer available demographic goals as may be established by the government of Canada from time to time in respect of the size, rate of growth, structure and geographic distribution of the Canadian population." This introduced for the first time the right to family reunification and humanitarian measures in favour of refugees. With its entry into force in April, 1978, the new law would later be amended more than 30 times, until the final substitution with the Immigration and Refugee Protection Act of 2002. This act decisively marked Canadian immigration policy on the world stage as a model of rationality and fairness.

However, the concrete realization of reforms brought about by multiculturalism and the politics of the "just society" did not happen quickly, nor was it devoid of conflicts and contradictions. What's more, among the priorities of the government there was always the achievement of full national sovereignty. Trudeau was able to act as historic necessity required, making a success of almost everything that constituted his own personal and collective dream for Canada's future. His popularity reached overseas, not only as a result of actions considered remarkable for those times, such as his support for the Cuban government of Fidel Castro or his being the first Western leader to pay a visit to Peking (Beijing) and to establish diplomatic ties with the People's Republic of China. He would also raise a great stir with his tough resolve in suppressing the terrorist drift of the Quebec Separatists; the abolition of the death penalty; the drive to have, for the first time, a woman appointed Governor General, the Head of State; and the creation of the public oil company, Petro-Canada. Undoubtedly, for all that, history will record as the greatest masterpiece of Pierre Trudeau the attainment of constitutional autonomy and full national sovereignty. These two issues had for decades enlivened the cultural-political debate and ultimately required 14 years of action by the Canadian government, led by Trudeau, to become reality.

With the British North America Act of 1867, otherwise known as the "Constitution of 1867," the British parliament had approved a partial independence for the Canadian colonial territories, but reserved the ownership of foreign policy and control of legislative initiative of Canada for the United Kingdom. Therefore, to achieve what Lester Pearson had called "patriation" of the Constitution was a fundamental historical goal, albeit opposed by many, and in any case, was to be achieved through an infinite number of distinctions and different points of view.

The difficulties in reaching "patriation," both the internal ones and those interjected by the UK, were such and were so prolonged in time that, to have a clear idea, one need only to think of the complexity of the process by which it was possible to include in the Constitution, finally patriated, the Charter of Rights and Freedoms. Adopted in 1960, and inspired by the Universal Declaration of Human Rights proclaimed by the UN in 1948 and the European Convention for the Protection of Human Rights of 1950, this Constitution proclaimed, among other things, the right to equality before the law, the right to one's own native language, freedom of thought, religion, press, assembly, association. However, this law was not binding for the provincial governments, and could only exert full effect on becoming an integral part of the Constitution. To this end, in 1980, a wide public consultation was undertaken, through which several changes to the 1960 text were introduced. But much opposition was still being interposed, until with the Kitchen Accord an end was put to the lengthy negotiations that would finally give the green light to "patriation."

The Kitchen Accord was signed on the night of November 4, 1981 in the kitchen of a government building in Ottawa between Jean Chrétien, the Federal Minister of Justice, and the Attorneys General of Ontario and Saskatchewan. The agreement conceded to the provincial governments the ability to implement certain parts of the Charter of Rights and Freedoms gradually. Trudeau knew that there would be no other way to end the "patriation" process, and so he accepted the compromise. Finally, for the last time, he asked the United Kingdom to adopt a Canadian law: the Canada Act of 1982, which was the only law of the UK ever written in both English and French.

The Canada Act, containing the new Canadian Constitution, including the Charter of Rights and Freedoms, was signed on April 17, 1982, in Ottawa by Queen Elizabeth II and countersigned by Pierre Trudeau. The "patriation" of the Constitution was a done deal; the former colony of Canada and its dependence upon the British parliament was relegated to a memory of the past. The Canadian nation took flight toward new horizons of its history. Now, the only legal bond with the old mother country remained the purely formal role of the Head of State which was reserved for the Queen or King of the United Kingdom. After all the innovations introduced through his initiative, a reporter asked Trudeau why he had not included the final piece, removing the symbolic role of the Head of State left to the British Crown. The answer was the ultimate testament to the political and diplomatic wisdom that made Trudeau such a unique case in Canadian history: "Why engage in a difficult and unpleasant discussion on a topic that brings nothing to anyone and from which no one takes anything?"

Despite the fact that Trudeau had been away from public life for 16 years, his funeral, held in Montreal on October 3, 2000, after five days of national mourning, was one of Canada's most memorable events, for the immense public participation and for the emotion which was felt throughout the country. Among the mourners, there were numerous personalities present: artists and Heads of State from around the world, including Cuban President Fidel Castro and former U.S. President Jimmy Carter. His son Justin Trudeau ended his eulogy with these words: "The woods are lovely, dark and deep. He has kept his promises and earned his sleep. Je t›aime, papa."

FIVE

Italian post-war immigration

I<small>N</small> 1834, the small settlement of York on the northern shore of Lake Ontario, a little more than a military fort, is renamed Toronto and proclaimed "city." There are just 9,254 inhabitants. By 1901, the inhabitants have grown to 208,000, to which must be added 30,000 in the suburbs. The growth is slow but steady. In 1951 there are 676,000 residents and in the suburbs there are another 442,000. In the space of little more than a century, the small initial population has increased more than a hundred times. The acceleration then becomes frenetic: in 1971 there are already more than two million inhabitants. In the early years of the third millennium, finally, the population of Greater Toronto exceeds 5,500,000.

A considerable part of Toronto's population growth is due to the influx of immigrants, of which the Italian component is one of the most relevant. In the 30 years, from 1947-1977, 430,000 Italians arrived in Canada, most of whom settled in the Greater Toronto area. Therefore, one can well understand what a great phenomenon the building activity has been in the second half of the 20th century, constructing homes, public, industrial and commercial buildings, roads, aqueducts, sewers and more. Beginning in the years immediately following the end of the Second World War, the Canadian economy gallops ahead and encourages immigration from Europe. The construction industry is the driving force of development.

A great number of immigrants from Italy found work in that industry. The majority of this workforce was made up of young and not so young lacking any kind of experience. But there were also the skilled masons and carpenters who would be the key to technological innovation and the aesthetic quality of the spectacular works by which the face of Toronto is completely redesigned, becoming the wonder of modernity appreciated by any visitor. The Italian immigrants in the post-war years, however, encountered extremely difficult times, marked by serious hardships of adjustment, and complicated by periodic economic crises, characterized by bitter struggles for the attainment of basic rights and unionization.

The date of March 17, 1960 is the watershed between a "before" and "after" in the condition of the majority of Italian immigrants. It is the tragic beginning of the path that would lead to a revolution in the construction industry in Toronto, resulting in the birth of a genuine trade union movement and of progressive improvements in pay and working conditions. The "before" meant sacrifices, often inhumane, defamatory discrimination, and savage exploitation by employers without any scruples. Many of the Italians arrived in this country never having known city life. They brought along cultural baggage that was less than minimal, and were completely oblivious to English and to other languages spoken in Canada. Their mastery of their own Italian language was even problematic and, of course, they were penniless, ill fed, and worse, ill clothed. For the most part, they were without a job. Aside from the inevitable but statistically modest number of cases of deviant and delinquent tendencies, they were armed only with stubborn honesty, a fierce desire to work, a willingness to submit to any work-related harassment, and a desperate need to send some money to the families left behind in Italy.

In their free time, Italian immigrants enjoyed the few distractions offered by a visit to the local bars set up by enterprising countrymen, and by gathering to exchange small talk on the sidewalks in front of these taverns, with fellow adventurers. But even in these innocent practices that were brought from the villages of origin, the Italians met with hostility which to them was inconceivable. The police, accustomed to the more conservative Anglo-Saxon practices, moved them along because stopping to chat in the street was not considered something for respectable people to be doing. The women were now beginning to appear in the streets, in the shops or in the church, but only after months and perhaps years of fearful self-segregation in the home. As for the workforce, Italian immigrants were generally underpaid, subjected to exhausting shifts, exposed to all kind of risks, and without any form of protection.

Then came the laborious, slow and often dramatic beginning of the "after" phase. It all started on the 17th of March, 1960. A tunnel was being dug in the locality known as Hogg's Hollow, under the Don River, along the route of the aqueduct intended to serve the then burgeoning urbanization of North York. Five Italian workers were engaged on the night shift: Pasquale Allegrezza, 26, Giovanni Corriglio, 46, Giovanni Fusillo, 27, the brothers Alessandro and Guido Mantella, one 25 and the other 23. The tunnel completely caved in on top of them. It took three days to recover their bodies. This was one of the many fatalities that for years hit the labourers, mostly Italian, operating in the multitude of active construction sites in Toronto. Moreover, it was not the last: soon after, on May 31st, in a dockyard between Weston Rd and Coulter Av, the digger Gabriel Carbone, father of five children, was buried alive under a landslide. While it was neither the first nor the last, Hogg's Hollow was the on-site job accident that more than any other jolted the conscience and agitated the stagnant waters of resignation of working people, and the tranquil life of the upper classes.

What happened at Hogg's Hollow was an announced carnage: the inadequacies of the site had long been established by inspections. The contractor and the administrators of the construction site were not qualified for the management of underground work; much less were the young and inexperienced workers involved in the operation. The area being excavated was greatly at risk, it being friable on account of its location beneath a water course. In the tunnel there was no source of lighting, nor any phone service. Neither fire extinguishers nor first aid and safety equipment existed. As for the workers, they toiled without the aid of mechanical tools but only with pick and shovel. They had not been fitted with flashlights or safety helmets, safety shoes or gloves or any kind of protective clothing. During the night, defective welding sparked a fire at the entrance of the tunnel. The blaze caused extensive collapsing inside. No immediate help came. The medical examiner, Dr. D.K. McAteer, used the term "merciless" in defining the behaviour of those responsible for the construction site: "The attitude of the management towards the safety of the individual worker can be described as no less than callous."

For the English language newspapers it was no longer possible to pretend that nothing had happened. The Ontario government set up a commission of inquiry into safety on construction sites, even though no concrete results would follow. However, the prominence of the news reports and the constant reverberation of word of mouth, while provoking waves of horror among the population, stirred the immigrants' anger which for some time had smouldered beneath the embers of resignation. Meetings and assemblies became increasingly more crowded at the Italo-Canadian Recreation Club of Brandon Ave. Frenzied protests and individual outbursts, a little at a time, gave way to a rudimentary para-union organization. In less than four months there was enough knowledge, energy and discipline necessary to take action.

The first strike of construction workers in Toronto began on the 1st of August. It was an illegal strike, because it was not declared in accordance with the applicable procedural rules, and this meant having to face the restraining stand of the police. However, the Brandon Group, that is, the trade union organization that was taking shape on Brandon Avenue, was fully aware of how the illegality of the strike would not influence in the slightest the determination of the mass of desperate and displaced immigrant workers on construction sites in Toronto. The event was very unusual and gained massive coverage by the English-speaking press, which defined it as "the revolt of the immigrants." From the beginning, there were numerous arrests that incited angry reactions often resulting in violence involving assaults and ravages in the yards where the strike did not obtain recruits. For its part, the police did not spare the use of unrestrained brutality. After three weeks, the strike ended with the signing of an embryonic collective bargaining agreement.

Soon, however, what had been hailed as a success for resolute action led by the Brandon Group began to look like a failure. Contractors who had signed the collective agreement were protesting against the unfair competition of colleagues who, not having signed, continued to pay lower wages and also impose heavier work shifts. On the other hand, the workers not affiliated with the Brandon Group rumbled about having to continue to endure less optimal working conditions than those who had gone on strike. As to the settlement of compensation, a significant number of the contractors were not paying, and if they did, it was with cheques rejected by the banks because they lacked the funds. This cruel practice enjoyed immunity protection by some very obliging legislation. In fact, after putting into circulation a large amount of void cheques, the contractors declared bankruptcy, shockingly, leaving employees and vendors on the streets. Soon after, they would resume the same activities with impunity, managed by shrewdly acquiring a new and different name.

Moreover, the consistently distinctive trait in the behaviour of employers was the insensitivity towards workers, especially immigrants. The tragedy of Hogg's Hollow placed before the public eye the practice of engaging people in dangerous jobs without training them and without providing them with the most elementary precautions. Now other forms of insensitivity emerged. The stark reality was that those people were treated as if they were inanimate objects, easily replaced when they broke down or became irreparably injured. Those months after the strike were therefore among the worst, spent in the grip of severe winter weather and acute shortages of money, work, and prospects for the future.

After a long and frigid winter of despair between the end of 1960 and the beginning of 1961, conditions developed such that the time was right for a second and more decisive action. The new strike began on May 29, 1961 and proved to be "long and hard," as had been antici- pated in the preparatory meetings. This also was an illegal strike. The workers were exasperated, but this time at least they were not alone: several contractors stood by them, as they themselves were tired of a system that required them to produce more and more, and more rap- idly, in the face of steadily declining profits. With each passing day, the pickets in front of construction sites became more aggressive. The dam- age to work in progress and to the equipment increased, as did the ram- pant arrests and ill-treatment by the police. The owners of construction companies, alarmed not only by the strike of Italian workers but also from the increasing allegiance of workers of other ethnic groups and the support provided by several contractors, asked the federal Minister of Immigration to crush the unrest by resorting to the deportation of immigrant strikers. The intimidation did not even put a dent in the per- sistence of the protest; indeed, it inspired more militancy. Newspapers shouted new headlines every day, estimating that from 5,000 to 9,000 workers were on strike, and pointing out that as a consequence, this inactivity would stall the construction of 20,000 buildings. Much of the city was paralyzed because of the marches, the workers picketing and because of police road blocks. Mass arrests and harsh sentences could not prevail.

At one point, dozens of wives, mothers, girlfriends and sisters, many with children in their arms or being held by the hand, started a sit-in in front of the jail where their relatives were imprisoned. The news shook everyone, and began to stir the social conscience, giving way to a wide- spread feeling of sympathy for the strikers, who were finally beginning to be considered as human beings, subjected to severe exploitation and humiliation. By the sixth week, both the physical state and the will of the strikers were exhausted. What's more, the economic difficulties put at risk the chance of survival for themselves and for their families. It was hard to imagine a positive outcome now, after the protracted state of agitation. The time finally came to gamble on an initiative capable of renewing the community's determination and hope. This initiative worked and got the desired result: a call for a rally in support of the strike saw 17,000 workers cram the stands of the Canadian National Exhibition. Important leaders of the labour movement attended as well, such as David Archer, president of the Ontario Federation of Labour, and Larry Sefton, national director of the United Steelworkers Union. Not only the trade unionists, but also members of different religions took turns at the microphone. The clergy included Rev. David Summers of the Toronto Religion and Labour Council; Rabbi Abraham Feinberg; and the Rev. Arthur Grunand of the Presbyterian Church. They were outraged at the way immigrants employed in the construction industry were being treated. They came to express solidarity. Toronto had never before witnessed such a thing.

Finally, after seven weeks, the second major strike ended, but this time the results were slight compared to the reasons for which the battle was fought. One of the unsolved fundamental problems was the difference in treatment between unionized and non-unionized workers. Improvements in wages and work hours were recognized only for union members who had signed the agreements. A major obstacle was the opposition of the major trade unions to support the legislative initiative that would give a final positive outcome to the year-long struggle: same pay and same hours for everyone, regardless of whether one was a member of the unions or not. The big trade unions, almost all established in Washington, which had barely accepted the initiatives and successes of the Brandon Group, were careful not to lose power, which drew strength from the number of workers represented and the resulting revenue secured by membership fees. The reasoning of the union leaders was simple: if the government starts to protect the interests of the workers, why would the workers need to turn to us?

Throughout the highs and lows, between one negotiation and another, and from obstacle to obstacle, the statutory provision was finally approved in August, 1963, having as its basis the substantive issues of the first collective agreement of August 10, 1960, which had been signed by unions and contractors. At this point it is worth recalling some of the names of leaders who grew to prominence during the strike. There was Charles Irvine, then an international vice president of the Operative Plasterers and Cement Masons International Union. He had chosen as his main "lieutenant" Bruno Zanini, of Friulian origin, a man of great charisma among workers. With his extraordinary eloquence he succeeded in moving masses, despite his 'italiese', i.e. a language mix of Friulian dialect, Italian, and colloquial English. Zanini also had a controversial and enigmatic personality. At the end of the strike he was arrested and convicted of fraud, although he would always proclaim his innocence. Another player of importance was Giancarlo Stefanini, a young Friulian just arrived from Italy. He embraced the strike with youthful enthusiasm, to the point that he was arrested for resisting an officer. His initial sentence of six months was reduced upon appeal to three. After the strike, Stefanini joined Local 183 of the Laborers International Union (LIUNA) where he spent his entire career as a unionist, eventually becoming the leader, as Business Manager for many years. Stefanini recently published a book entitled *Strike: History of an Italian in Canada* (Ed. Lavoro: Rome, 2014). In this book, he gives his recollections of a half century of Canadian labour history.

Another leader to emerge, also from Friuli, was Marino Toppan. Although he never reached the peak of power, he spent many years of service with Local 506 of the Laborers International Union, where he was the acting president for a short time. For 20 years, Marino Toppan hosted a radio program in Italian, called The Voice of Labour. After retirement, he put all his recollections into a book with the title, *The Voice of Labour* (Toronto: 2004). Finally, I will mention Frank Colantonio, who was a major organizer with the Carpenters Union. He was from Molise, a true gentleman with high moral principles. He never compromised his integrity, contributing intense work in the community with the Italian Immigrant Aid Society, and with the International Institute of Metropolitan Toronto. Colantonio also produced a book of memoirs, entitled *From the Ground Up* (Toronto: 1997).

The events of the sixties which I have taken some time to describe may seem far-fetched to those who did not live through them, compared to the conditions of the present time. That was, indeed, the reality, and in the thick of that reality tens of thousands of Italians continued to arrive in Canada, planning to remain here and become full citizens of this country. After those early sixties, the role of the Italians which had been fundamental, since it was they who had begun the unionization of construction workers, gradually began to lose precedence. Indeed, the Italians were literally crushed by the preponderance of the Irish, who were by now as many as the Italians in number and, more importantly, spoke the dominant English language. Moreover, even in union branches where the Italians were in the majority, the Irish did whatever they wanted with absolute authority, jostling to ensure benefits from which others were excluded. For example, in the case of Local 183, one of the union locals which had more clout, the Italians were 80% of those enrolled, but the 20% Irish members paid very little attention to the voice of the majority.

Only much later were the Italians within the Canadian labour movement finally able to attain a substantial revival of their ability to propose initiatives. The protagonists of that phase succeeded in achieving for Italian Canadians the level of representation legitimized by the general recognition of their professional and social prestige as well as the broad consensus of opinion gained from other ethnic groups. Achieving these results was neither easy nor painless. The journey might have been more arduous and lengthy had there not been other considerable changes in social conditions. Rebellion against the old order exploded on college campuses in the United States and then swept across the West. In Canada, the major change was the advent of Trudeau at the helm.

The events of 1968 that started a new course of Canadian politics also complicated a most decisive moment. Trudeau, who had emerged a few years earlier within the Liberal Party, left behind a university professorship in jurisprudence. In 1965, he was elected as a member of the House of Commons. Then in 1967, he was appointed to Cabinet as the Minister of Justice where he garnered much respect and popularity. In April, 1968, at the Liberal Party Convention, he was chosen as the new leader of the party. Soon afterwards, in the federal elections held on June 25, 1968, he would become Prime Minister. He obtained a significant majority, which over the years made it possible for him to lead Canada towards an epic transformation of the socio-cultural system and of the structure of the state.

On April 3, 1968, two days before the opening of the Liberal Party Convention, the *Corriere Canadese* came out with a headline on the top of the front page that, surprisingly, abandoned the usual detachment with which this influential Canadian newspaper in Italian usually reported the events relating to the community. It discussed openly the "problems of democracy" within the construction Local 183. It denounced the excessive power of the Irish who controlled the Local. It argued that the bulk of the members, 2,500 Italians out of a total of 3,150 members, were deprived of any opportunity to play an important role due to the location and dates of the meetings.

In fact, the meetings were always called for 8 pm on Fridays, and took place in a downtown area far removed from a district where the workers lived. The newspaper reported that the Italians had hoped to hold these same meetings on Sunday, a day which would allow them to participate in large numbers and, consequently, be more influential. However, the paper refrained from alluding to a much simpler explanation. The Italian workers knew very well that the intent of convening at such time and place was primarily to hinder their participation. The meetings were held at the end of the work week, rushed in a matter of a few minutes so that they might then enjoy bingeing on beer in one or more of the many pubs scattered in the area.

During April of 1968, the situation within Local 183 was becoming too hot to handle. Events were fomenting and the factitious equilibrium that had been achieved began showing alarming signs of collapse. Three Italian workers had been fired by the Redfer Construction Company. In the eyes of their fellow countrymen, those layoffs had appeared absolutely unjust. Biagio Di Giovanni came forward brandishing accusations, not only within Local 183 but also to the media, that the directors of the same Local 183 had not defended the fired workers. In so doing, he drew upon himself the wrath of the union leaders who decreed a life expulsion from the organization.

It was the Easter period, but there was neither peace nor serenity among the Italian construction workers. The *Corriere Canadese*, which at that time had not yet become a daily but was still a weekly paper, issued a front-page headline in 8 columns, in the edition of April 17, reporting the event held in support of Biagio. Hundreds of Italian workers had gathered in front of the headquarters of Local 183. Above the sea of protesters soared a variety of signs with expressions of protest. Soon afterwards, in procession, everyone moved to the St. Clair Cinema that had been booked in order to carry out the final stage of the event. The keynote speech was given by Odoardo Di Santo, not yet a parliamentarian, but even then a combative leader of the community in the role of editor-in-chief of the *Corriere Canadese*. "We must be united," he said. "The union sentence against Di Giovanni is as grim and merciless as to have only one precedent in the trade union history of North America, the facts of which are much more serious and justified. Firing him is a warning to all Italians to not raise their head."

Animated discussions took place on what to do about the umpteenth meeting of Local 183 for the following Friday, the 19th. In the end everyone agreed on the need to participate en masse, despite the sacrifice entailed by the date and place of the meeting. It was necessary to go both in order to enforce the rules of democracy and to bring about two significant gains: the revocation of the expulsion of Biagio and the move to Sundays for all future meetings.

The meeting was convened on Friday, April 19, in the hall of the Labour Lyceum at Spadina Avenue. The Hall was overcrowded, and the meeting lasted just long enough to get started. On April 24 the *Corriere Canadese* headlined a 7 column headline on the front page: "Violence prevents Local 183 from the exercise of a democratic vote." There were 500 Italians and 100 or so Irish. The latter immediately went on the attack, "a brutal aggression," writes the *Corriere Canadese*. The Italians reacted swiftly, with the same level of ferocity. However, the acerbity of the clash is noteworthy: chairs were smashed; people were punched, kicked and bludgeoned. The police, of course, were alerted, but refrained from intervening, except for the final stage, when the officers finally undertook to quell the tempers.

The days that followed were full of frantic negotiations and exasperated tensions. We turned to the central union office, which had its headquarters in Washington, asking for the re-establishment of the statutory rules and the restoration of civil functionality within Local 183. First, it was necessary to reconvene the meeting of the members, but the senior management of Local 183 employed a strategy that aimed at undermining the strength of the Italians and discouraging their willingness to participate; a date was at first fixed, then moved several times. Likewise, different locations were chosen for the meetings, each time farther and farther away from where there was a high concentration of Italians.

Finally, the meeting was held May 19 at the Lansdowne Cinema, on a Sunday at 10 am. The Italians logistic requests had been met, as well as the revocation of the sanction against Biagio Di Giovanni. There were more than 1,000 participants at the meeting, but everything proceeded quietly, and no one wanted to rehash the particulars of the recent past events. The leadership remained what it was, at least for the time being. After all, Irish and Italian had worked for years side by side with a great spirit of camaraderie. They shared similar adversities and had common aspirations.

The mediation of the central union office in Washington had paid off and no one was going to continue to keep the situation at the union in a state of tension, when of far greater concern were the problems to be faced with the employers. The hype around the story of Local 183 dissipated and newspapers, including the English language ones, moved away from the emphasis given to the days of rage, towards complete disinterest. A few days later there was another burst of sensationalism, as a result of yet another fatal accident at a construction site that had taken the lives of three Italian workers. This brought attention back, both from within the union and from the media, to the old issue of safety and the prevention of occupational hazards.

However, the tumultuous days of April, 1968, seemed to extinguish the modest success and gave the impression of having come up with a very meagre gain. Other events took precedence in the general public's attention, such as the futuristic outlook that appeared on the horizon with the announcement of Trudeau as Prime Minister. The campaign and then the triumphant outcome of the federal election of June 25 would expedite definitively the policy reforms designed by the new Prime Minister. In addition, abruptly, there was the assassination of Bobby Kennedy.

The true extent of the success resulting from the April events in Local 183 could be measured in the medium and long term. From that point on, the union meetings were held in venues always located in Italian neighbourhoods, always on a Sunday, always in the morning and with the complete facility for Italian to be spoken. All this made possible a large, active and constant participation. Gradually this allowed awareness to mature regarding their rights and obligations, and made possible the growth of self-management skills of the individual, and thus of the contribution of these improvements to the formation of collective decisions. Thus, step by step, all of the workers, not just those of Local 183, gained self-awareness and self-esteem. They learned to develop proposals and initiatives of general interest; they gained an aptitude for leadership; they were able to disentangle the intricacies of democratic processes; and, finally, they were able to grasp the opportunities offered by elections. After April, 1968, they won the election in Local 183 and in almost all the other locals. Subsequently, local affirmation was cast on a much larger scale, allowing the talent and skills of Italo-Canadian workers to gain positions of importance in all trade union organizations throughout the country.

When the time came, the Italians peacefully relinquished power to the new majority made up of Portuguese workers. Today, it is gratifying to see how all the different groups can work together with a united front, which has greatly improved working conditions and labour relations. However, the struggle in the union movement was the first major breakthrough of the Italian community in the quest for greater participation and power-sharing in Canadian society at large.

SIX

Notables and Wannabes:
the Birth and Development of Associations

I<small>N</small> 1964, the sociologist Edith Ferguson, in her book *Newcomers in Transition,* described the community of Italian origin as the most numerous and the most disorganized. The community did not take offence at this sharp but stimulating analysis offered by Ferguson's book. Instead, the critique contributed to a growing awareness of the role and ability of Italians. Thus the first representative body of broad substance, FACI (Federation of Italian Associations and Clubs), came about, from which will then emerge the National Congress of Italian-Canadians and, gradually, all the other entities within the Italian community. Among these, the Centro Scuola e Cultura Italiana, which will rise from a philosophy all its own, free from the traditional logic of assistance and nostalgia of the usual immigrant organizations.

For decades the community had lived quietly, driven by the singular goal that had them moving to Canada: economic betterment. Toward the mid-60s such a goal had been partially achieved, or was within reach. A new wave of immigrants was arriving from Italy with a higher level of education and greater social awareness. At the same time, many of the children of the previous immigrants had grown up in Canada with a different outlook on life, and a different concept of social scale. This was to change radically the make-up of the community. In fact, it would give life to our own "Quiet Revolution." A new middle class was emerging, made up of professional and business people, and a white- and blue-collar working class was ready and eager to speak up. It was not long before the different social groups came into conflict.

The traditional value of "peaceful living" gave way to confronta- tion. On one hand there was the Old Guard made up of the so-called "Notables" and the "Wannabes"; on the other hand, everyone else, albeit with considerable diversification. The "Notables" were those who had capital and economic strength and, consequently, they held and exercised power. To describe them in a more obvious but perhaps more effective way, they were the "masters" or, when they spiced up their role with pomposity and bombastic rhetoric, the "braggarts." The "Wannabes" were those who "want to be," otherwise known as the "parvenues." They were the ones who, fresh from economic success, aspired to ascend the social ladder and gain power. In short, they also wanted to become "Notables," rather pathetic social climbers by reason of their aspirations.

The "Notables" considered themselves the natural representatives of the Italian community, but these self-proclaimed leaders and spokes- men often stirred up disagreements within the community. The "nou- veaux riches," who were even more annoying than the "prominent," could only boast of their recent rapid enrichment, exhibit brazen arro- gance borne out of their often shocking ignorance, and were nothing if not populists and demagogues.

"Notables" and "Wannabes" live separated from the community, in expensive neighbourhoods, and associate with people and places that are not easily accessed. They do not always get along with one another and, in truth, the former "Notables" detest the "Wannabes" and these, the lat- ter, envy the great social prestige of the "Notables." However, they sup- ported each other in a big way, when it came to preventing the "others" from gaining increased awareness of themselves and of their electoral importance. That would allow these "others" to destroy the elites' role as privileged authorities. It seems obvious to note that the "Notables" and the "Wannabes" always found themselves allies in thwarting the democratic needs/requirements emerging in the Italian community.

When the Italians in Toronto began to become more aware of themselves, of their significant force, of the increasing importance that they were assuming in the moral and material building of the country, and the prestige that the community finally began to enjoy in the national context, then the move towards a more united expression began to spread, and the desire to assert that identity grew. Until then the Italians had tried to disguise their identity to gain the approval of the Anglo-Saxon majority. The "Notables" and "Wannabes" had cared nothing for the new initiatives, nor felt any need to change their attitude. Among the entities beginning to understand that times were changing was the Catholic Church, which grasped the importance of identity, and set out to provide a new framework for parish work. Creating the Italian-Canadian Pastoral Commission signalled a change in the hegemony of the Church within the Archdiocese of Toronto.

These were times of intense debates, impassioned meetings, fervent development, both theoretical and constructive. All this, of course, occurred within the context of renewal in Canadian politics that would result in assuming the concept of multiculturalism. These were the seventies and early eighties, peak years in the creation of the new Canada and in the vitality of the Italian-Canadian community and its fervour for associations. In this context it became clear that the traditional strong point of the "Notables" and "Wannabes," that is, the cultivation of folklore and the celebration of the glories of the ancient homeland, was no longer enough. It would be necessary instead to address the real problems and needs of the community: education, citizenship, the rights of immigrant workers, overcoming discrimination, improving economic and social conditions, access of immigrants to posts of government representation in public institutions, and full recognition of the validity of the equation, "equal obligations – equal rights" for all.

The thrust towards a new type of association arose, a drive towards the creation of a federation with which all the Italian-Canadians could identify and through which they could develop a synergy capable of catalysing the major initiatives of the community. The impetus came from a wide variety of groups, from associations of regions and towns to cultural and religious ones; from educational organizations and trade unions to those groups involved in assistance and professional care for pensioners, disabled people, and youth.

Between the end of 1969 and the first months of 1970 countless meetings were held and the debate was intense. It began with a discussion of the desirability of a new entity and gradually evolved to considering the aims, the programs, the name and the regulations. We met in what had been the Casa d'Italia, a building erected during the fascist years, then confiscated by the Canadian government at the beginning of World War II. It was then returned to the Italian-Canadian community, who used it to establish COSTI (Italian Organisational Centre for Technical Schools). Ultimately, due to a legal technicality, the building became the property of the Italian State, even though it had been built with the money and the sacrifices of immigrants.

The great debate came to bear fruit: at last, the text of the statute was written and approved and it was agreed to name the new society The Federation of the Italian Associations and Clubs, which soon became for everyone, simply "FACI." In April, 1970, the founding meeting was held at the Italian Recreation Club, the charter was approved and elections were held to select an Executive Committee. The officers so allocated were: Lorenzo Petricone, President; Elio Costa and Elio Madonia as Vice Presidents; and Alberto Di Giovanni, Odoardo Di Santo, Dante Francescut, Laureano Leone, Carmine Nepa, Rino Pellegrino, Bruno Suppa, Sigismondo Zonni as Members at Large.

There were some disagreements, but the Directors set to work immediately, dealing with problems of primary importance to the community, and soon gaining positive results. Safety on the job became the major issue. A real estate boom was under way, and contractors gave scant attention to injury prevention and accidents which all too often were fatal. There was nothing to be done, however, because the workers were always accorded the blame, even by the unions. FACI chose to focus its work on lobbying in favour of the injured and their families. The success achieved was something no one had dared hope for. We also dealt with the issue of Vocational Schools, to which so many children of Italian descent were assigned, depriving them of the possibility of applying for entrance to education for the professional level. This matter, and the radical transformation which brought about change, are dealt with in other parts of this book. Another important issue was citizenship. The Executive worked hard with both the provincial and federal governments to promote the acceleration of bureaucratic procedures. Among other things, they managed to obtain a reduction in the minimum period of residence in order to become a Canadian citizen, from five to three years.

The achievements attained through the activities of FACI were greeted enthusiastically not only within the community, but also gained acknowledgement from government agencies. The Municipality of Toronto recognized FACI as the only entity truly representative of Italian Canadians. The general consensus of the authorities seemed to be that they were satisfied to have available a stable, scrupulous and reliable voice. A sign of this confidence was the provision of a head office with a symbolic rent. It was a solid and spacious building at 756 Ossington Avenue, where it was possible to locate not only the FACI offices, but a well-stocked library, spaces for recreation and entertainment, and various rooms for meetings and cultural activities. In short, we started a new process, autonomous and irreversible, which would enable self-management at all levels of the community, changing profoundly its ability to act within the overall social context.

We became ever more tightly integrated into the socio-cultural Canadian fabric, on the one hand aware of our own historical identity and on the other also proud to contribute to building a new nation. As the dichotomy between being Italian and being Canadian was gradually overcome, the mentality of being "Canadian of Italian culture" began to grow. This enhanced our ability to act and achieve new goals independently, by virtue of our own determination and a wealth of experience, no longer relying on hearsay but gained first-hand. At one

point, however, in the course of this progression which was so innovative and compelling, something happened that could have ultimately
complicated the already less than ideal relations with the diplomatic
authorities of the motherland. The year was 1971, and the Ministry of
Foreign Affairs in Rome issued the order for the creation of Consular
Advisory Committees chaired by consuls in the various countries of
Italian emigration.

The Consul General then in office was told that a new body representative of Italian Canadians, especially if imposed from above, would
certainly have generated a conflict with the existing associations which
originated locally. Unfortunately, the attempt to dissuade anyone from
fragmenting the community again was in vain. The Consul General
convened a meeting at the Casa d'Italia. The meeting was overcrowded
and the confrontation between opposing factions reached rather harsh
tones. The showdown culminated with 90% of those present turning against the establishment of a Consular Committee. Nevertheless,
the Consul General, in defiance of so much opposition, formed the
Committee, appointing members from his closest circle. That was only
the prelude to a state of tension, often marked by bitter contrasts, which
would drag on for several years. The situation finally abated somewhat.
Various initiatives aimed at establishing a constructive dialogue followed, along with a few adjustments that gave regulatory operational
usefulness to the Consular Committees. Above all, for the composition
of the Committees, the democratic process was introduced, thereby
electing its members from the community.

It should be noted that relations with the diplomatic authorities varied depending on the individuals entrusted with the role of Consul
General. When wisdom prevailed, even in the face of legal obstacles,
solutions to accommodate were almost always found. Toronto has seen
more than one Consul General endowed with an aptitude for dialogue
in relations with the local community. Other consuls have engaged several times in trying to turn back the clock of social history. Two, in particular, were anxious to ensure the leadership of the Italian-Canadian
community and the control of people and organizations by creating

a sort of supermarket of awards: knighthoods were bestowed on any person who assured him full support in his strategy to reconstitute the dependence of the community on consular power. The thirst for power went so far as to control the organizations of young Italian Canadians of the second and third generations. In the end, that strategy failed miserably.

In conclusion, one cannot ignore that, in those years when we so laboriously attempted to create a new model of community representation based on democratic structures, it seems that the motherland did all in its power to prevent this from happening. Instead of addressing issues regarding the new reality, such as the promotion of Italian culture and Italian innovation, the basic attitude of many in the diplomatic corps remained anchored to the old paternalistic ways, which the Italian Canadians needed less and less. The emigrants and their descendants were not considered as culturally evolved citizens capable of promoting the rich culture of Italy, its language, and the "Made in Italy" abroad. Rather they were seen as a docile mass on which to bestow superficial patronage.

Going back to FACI and the community, in 1972, there was a change in the executive. The elections resulted in a neat split between the progressive and the conservative components: the latter was able to elect Elio Madonia as President. Although Madonia was a reformist, hostility towards him was the decisive factor for the birth of what would soon become the prime organization of the Italian community: the National Congress of Italian Canadians.

The idea of the Congress was the consequence of the drive and input of the federal MP Carletto Caccia. A prominent personality in the Liberal Party, Caccia was born in Milan, obtained a degree in forestry sciences in Vienna in 1954, and arrived in Canada in 1955. In 1959, he was among the founders of COSTI and, shortly afterwards, embraced political life. He was a supporter of the "melting pot," one who believed in recognizing the dominant culture rather than working to safeguard the inherited culture of the immigrants. In fact, he changed his first name to Charles, only to return to the original Carletto several years later, when "multiculturalism" had become the new civil religion of Canada. Caccia was always very progressive, consistently taking a stand against backwardness and the obtuseness of the old establishment. He earned a loyal following among young people all over. Clever and charming, he had achieved the kind of success that opened a new era when, in 1966, he was elected City Councillor in Toronto, vying in a completely Anglophone constituency. Such an achievement had only one earlier precedent, Joseph Piccininni, who was born in Canada, while Caccia was born, grew up and was formed in Europe. After two terms at City Hall, he was a candidate in a constituency with a strong presence of voters of Italian origin, and was elected a Member of Parliament. Caccia was not the first Italian to sit on the benches of Parliament in Ottawa, because even before the Second World War there had been Badanai from North Bay and Macaluso from Hamilton, but he was certainly the one who was able to achieve greater status. First appointed Minister of Labour, he found no great success, but in his subsequent role of Minister of the Environment he proved himself, gaining the admiration of the whole nation. In 1974, during the crisis within FACI, Caccia was a politician of rank, very influential, with a clear vision and a high profile. It is understandable, then, that he could quickly determine the potential of the Congress of Italian-Canadians . At its founding, the first elected President of the Congress was Alfredo Campo, an oil industrialist, who was prominent in Montreal. At that point, we were all convinced that, faced with a new phenomenon, a reality clearly at odds with the FACI, Madonia would take revenge, unleashing a battle. Madonia, instead, brought about constructive and sincere cooperation between the Congress and FACI. He would subsequently want as his successor and President of FACI, Laureano Leone, politically apart from him, but someone with whom he had established a warm relationship of respect throughout the constructive dialogue to dispel the conflict within the Italian-Canadian community.

Leaving FACI behind, Madonia focused on becoming a member of the Ontario Legislature, nominated under the banner of the Conservative Party. The task proved more daunting than expected as the Italian-Canadian constituency in which he ran had traditionally voted for the Liberal Party or the NDP. In fact, he was not elected; his opponent, after all, was a real thoroughbred. That defeat brought Madonia to the completion of his short season as a politician and his return to full-time role of businessman in the field of soft drinks and milk, something which had always brought him satisfying results. Subsequently, he retired from business and opened an evangelical mission for the care of orphaned children in the Dominican Republic.

The "thoroughbred" winner of the election for the Ontario Legislature was Odoardo Di Santo, an authentic "Homo Politicus" who soon became a leading figure in Ontario public life. He was born in Rocca Pia, a town in Abruzzo, in 1934. Graduating in law from the University of Rome, he was also a professional journalist working for the newspaper *La Giustizia*. In the years 1965 to 1966 he directed the press office of the Minister of Industry, Edgardo Lami Starnuti, and in 1967 he emigrated to Toronto, where he was active as an investigative journalist. He gained notoriety as a result of his coverage of the extensive and serious pattern of workplace accidents.

Laureano Leone also came from Rocca Pia. He had been regional secretary for the Abruzzo region of ACLI (Christian Associations of Italian Workers), and in 1950 he set out for North America. Six years later he would graduate in pharmacy from the Detroit Institute of Technology. Once elected as president of FACI, he worked to bring about a merger with the National Congress, which quickly happened, making FACI the Toronto chapter of the Congress. He was himself elected President of the Congress in 1976 and again in 1978, working very well with the Trudeau government on many community projects, especially interacting with the ministers responsible for multiculturalism which had become the official policy of Canada.

That was a season distinguished by an extraordinarily intense collaborative effort between the Federal Government and the National Congress of Italian Canadians, not only with the issues concerning the community. Thanks to Leone's efforts, Italian Canadians were nominated as members of several government committees and, for the first time, two Italian Canadians had access to the coveted Senate seats: Pietro Rizzuto, an entrepreneur from Montreal; and Peter Bosa, a person of renowned integrity, an insurance broker who was elected several times as alderman of the City of York. He was well liked and respected in the community. At the end of his second term as Congress President, Leone opted to commit himself to politics and was subsequently elected Member of the Provincial Legislature in the Ontario Liberal Party. The National Congress of Italian Canadians continued to play an important role nationally, particularly throughout the years of presidency of two women of exceptional quality: Maria Minna and Annamarie Castrilli. Another effective president was Salvatore Amenda, a brilliant lawyer who was later appointed judge.

I must say that, despite some periods of confusion about its function and its activities, the Congress has never failed to fulfil those key words that were the fuel of its foundation: "The common good is the reason that unites us."

Inevitably, there comes a time of declining strength of the Congress, as a representative force of the community. This happens because a large number of Italian Canadians are present in many other organizations. A new direction commences, that of political success, which will see an increasing number of Italians elected to the various levels of government, from local to federal, up to the most senior ranks. Debates, discussions and decisions now move from the halls of the community buildings to municipal and legislative chambers. This topic will be examined in depth shortly.

SEVEN

Villa Colombo
and the Columbus Centre

B<small>EFORE LEAVING THE PRESIDENCY</small> of FACI and pursuing the electoral experience, Madonia put his successful business skills to good use, convincing the FACI Directors to establish a foundation for the advancement of a project backed by much of the community, namely the creation of a nursing home for the elderly. This foundation, named the Italian Canadian Benevolent Corporation, aimed at channelling the energy and resources of the wealthy members of the community towards philanthropic work, moving from the pursuit of structural reforms and focusing on charitable assistance. This produced two important achievements: Villa Colombo, the culturally welcoming residence for the elderly, and also the prestigious Columbus Centre. These projects both responded to the needs of the community at the time.

The Benevolent Corporation attracted a new group of "prominent" people and expanded the membership base and its activities. The more democratic representation of the community was put on hold, although it should be recognized that the new Benevolent Corporation, later to be called Villa Charities, was eventually able to leave behind a good deal of the original rhetoric of folklore and nostalgia. Asked to head the Benevolent Corporation was businessman Tony Fusco, of whom we shall speak further on. At this point, it should be reiterated that the long process started to create a new model of representation of the community based on democratic principles had to be sacrificed in order to achieve the more immediate results.

The idea of building the Villa Colombo home for the elderly was precisely the project which brought together both old and new immigrants, the Italian Canadians of a past immigration, whose way of seeing things was very different from that of the more recent immigrants who flocked here in the years following World War II. On April 15, 1971, the Italian Canadian Benevolent Corporation was officially founded. Besides John De Toro, a member of the older generation called to the role of Chairman, the members of the first Board of Directors, were one and the same as those of FACI: Elio Madonia, Lorenzo Petricone, Carmen Nepa, Odoardo Di Santo, Bruno Suppa, Laureano Leone, Elio Costa, Alberto Di Giovanni, Lorenzo Duso, Rino Pellegrina, Steve Perzia and Sigismondo Zonni.

Then, Madonia made the decisive move that would bring about the success of the initiative, developing the idea into reality. He moved to replace the newly-installed Board of Directors with a group of individuals who would be able to attract substantial financial support. The new team took office in September, 1971. They were John De Toro, John Carrier and Tony Fusco. It would eventually be the latter who firmly took hold of the reins, and gradually gained the support of the entire Italian-Canadian establishment, starting with Orey Fidani, Elvio and Angelo Del Zotto, Rudy Bratty, John Gennaro, and Marco Muzzo, among the top income earners in Canada.

On October 15, 1974, after a myriad of events that raised millions of dollars for the construction of the building, the foundation stone of Villa Colombo was put in place. Villa Colombo would be a structure designed in harmony with the taste of classical Italian architecture, and capable of accommodating approximately 200 senior residents. The inauguration of the facility in April, 1976, was a triumph that featured the involvement of international stars such as Gina Lollobrigida, Perry

Como, Rossano Brazzi and Jerry Lewis. The enthusiasm generated by Villa Colombo contributed to the construction of other residential buildings in the same area, as well as the impressive Columbus Centre, which opened in October, 1980.

With the transformation of York into Toronto, in 1834, after 40 years, the envoys of the British Monarchy in Toronto, as well as with Canberra, the Australian capital, made use of a word in the local dialect which was the equivalent of the English expression "meeting place." Thus, Toronto means "meeting place." With a name like "Toronto," the original inhabitants of the territories had chosen to indicate places actually appointed to an essential socio-cultural function, i.e., the periodic meetings between communities scattered over vast areas. However, the British intended anything but. For them, the "meeting places" had to be industrial sites, points of intersection for trade, and a central location for capital gains. Dangerous activities such as crowds of people and the public exchange of ideas were frowned upon; therefore, no "*piazzas*" or squares for cities were to be found in the colonies.

In truth, the three million residents of Toronto can only count on two squares that are not merely medians for separating traffic, which recall the concept of European, and particularly Italian, "piazza." These are spaces for children to play games, for promenading, for some idleness, conversation, the exchange of goods and ideas. Nathan Phillips Square in front of the City Hall is a location for concerts, markets, celebrations and, every New Year's Eve, an exhibit of ice sculptures. There is also the space covered by a giant glass vault which functions as the backbone to the Eaton Centre, the spectacular shopping mall which is in the centre of the city. Both these squares, one made in 1965 and the other in 1979, can be attributed not to the British footprint but to that of the new Toronto, largely the result of the pervasive influence on the local way of life that reflects the Italian good taste.

Some have suggested that the Columbus Centre in Toronto may be the third piazza. It's a brilliant theory, based not on its architectural form, but on the philosophy and function of the Centre. A sprawling complex, the Columbus Centre was built and financed by the Italian-Canadian community. The simple beauty of the red brick and glass exterior opens into an elegant marble interior. The Centre contains many features: art gallery, library, dance studios, classrooms, indoor swimming pool, gymnasium, sports fields, offices, restaurants and cafes. The Centre is frequented annually by thousands of people, including those who have no Italian heritage but are attracted to Italian style and hospitality.

So, yes, one can see Toronto's third piazza in the Columbus Centre! As a landmark it is famous, prestigious and admired by all with enthusiastic respect for the Italian creativity that created it. The founders wanted it "so that all Canadians have a new and very visible reason to continue seeing the Italians with respect and admiration ... so that it might instil a genuine feeling of pride and cultivate a sense of identity and belonging in the Italian Canadians ... so that it might generate a spirit of brotherhood and help all to grow together, cultivating the values of the Italian traditions in a sound and modern Canadian environment." Nothing could have been a better monument – useful and not rhetorical – erected to the memory of the thousands of Italians who arrived with cardboard suitcases tied with string, who had constructed both materially and socially their new country, Canada. Next to the Columbus Centre is Villa Colombo, the large and comfortable residence for the elderly that started the Italian-style urbanization of this part of the city. Both structures are governed by Villa Charities, an organization with a charitable status.

In its initial four years, the Columbus Centre, due to its architectural elegance and excellent facilities, constituted a significant attraction, for Italians as well as for a large part of the middle class in Toronto. Tony Fusco, a brilliant and successful entrepreneur, was the primary mover and shaker of these important community projects. Fusco had vision, and without him the Columbus Centre and Villa Colombo certainly would not have been built. However, his approach to cultural programs for the Centre was tied to amateur activities and nostalgia. I told him this, once, during a friendly encounter in the lobby of the Columbus Centre. He replied quoting an old proverb: "Let he who pays the piper call the tune." To which I answered, without malice: "Right, but what if he doesn't know how to play?" All the same, Tony Fusco deserves sincere gratitude for his many years of volunteer work on behalf of the community.

There was a period during which the cultural arts flourished, and achieved an outstanding reputation for the Columbus Centre. The turning point came in May of 1984, when the architect Renzo Pillon was President of the Board of Directors, and probably the best of those who have served in that role. Together with Executive Director Pal Di Iulio, they struck an agreement of close collaboration between Centro Scuola e Cultura Italiana and the Columbus Centre. They invited me, as Director of Centro Scuola, to take over the cultural programs in order to launch a vibrant agenda of diverse cultural activities.

Up until 2011, the Columbus Centre, along with its initial activities around gastronomy, fitness and business meetings, offered a flourishing number of artistic and educational programs. Choral music and sporting groups, activities for pre-school age to pre-conservatory music courses, all kinds of socializing initiatives for males and females of all ages were present at the Centre. There was a continuous stream of music concerts, theatre shows and art exhibitions. To cite an example, there was an exhibition of international nativity scenes every year at Christmas time. The influx of young people from the city schools recorded an average of 300 daily, for a total of 8000 between December 8 and January 6, the Feast of the Epiphany. Throughout the year the large entrance hall, study rooms and entertainment spaces, exhibition gallery and a well-supplied library were kept busy from morning to night by the ceaseless motion of young people who have always been the driving engine. Thanks to gatherings happening at lively restaurants, gyms and other facilities in operation, the Columbus Centre had become a meeting place, an open place, a true "piazza," Italian style, where we made dates to meet for conversation, exchange of news and spend some pleasant free time.

One could boast about the success of the cultural arts during this period, when dance students benefitted from teaching and coaching by dancer Roberto Campanella and former Principal Dancer Kimberly

Glassco, both of the National Ballet. There were high profile music teachers such as Fabio Mastrangelo and tenor Ermmano Mauro. The Palestrina Chamber Chorus presented concerts at the George Weston Recital Hall, in the North York Centre for the Performing Arts (now known as the Toronto Centre), and performed by invitation for His Holiness Pope John Paul II during the World Youth Days in Toronto. On tour in Italy, the Palestrina sang in the Pantheon in Rome, and the basilicas of St. Francis of Assisi, the Madonna of Loreto, and St. Antony of Padua, among other venues. Their level of achievement brought them to perform with the great Toronto Symphony Orchestra under the baton of Maestro Gianandrea Noseda, in Roy Thomson Hall, on November 16, 2002, before a full house of 2600.

At one point, however, the competition between the commercial and cultural sectors became a difficult one. It was obvious that, beyond a certain indifference towards the cultural vitality in the Columbus Centre on the part of the administration, what prevailed was the view that only recognizes what generates immediate revenue. This leads the investment in culture to sink to the bottom of any scale of values. Still, from the start, the intentions were good. It is notable that the annual fundraising Venetian Ball given by Villa Charities is always well- attended by the "crème de la crème" of Toronto's business tycoons. Tickets for this party come at a high price, but that is not likely to worry those with well-padded pockets. On average, the proceeds of this party bring in a profit margin of $1.5 million. On the strength of this, the potential is high for support in all areas, including the cultural arts.

I record with sadness the unfortunate developments in the direction of the Columbus Centre which have resulted in greatly diminished cultural activities in the halls of this popular centre. The Italian Canadian community and the entire city of Toronto deserve an organization of such great prestige not simply to function as a location for commercial services but to conduct itself as the heartbeat of creativity and artistry and the incubator of young talents, which it was able to be for many years in conjunction with Centro Scuola.

Pierre Trudeau, Canadian Prime Minister (1968–79, 1980–84), Senator Peter Bosa and Alberto Di Giovanni.

A delegation of Italian Canadians, headed by Gino Ventresca (far right), meet Paolo Rossi, top scorer at the 1982 World Cup in Spain won by Italy.

Italian Prime Minister Giulio Andreotti with Ontario Premier Bob Rae and Alberto Di Giovanni

The Italian President Oscar Luigi Scalfaro on an official visit to Canada (1997) with federal International Trade Minister Sergio Marchi, Ontario Minister of Economic Development, Trade and Tourism Al Palladini, and Alberto Di Giovanni.

Rome, Altare della Patria, September 6, 2002. Roberta Capua introduces Alberto Di Giovanni at the ceremony for the "Italians in the World" award, conferred by the Marzio Tremaglia Foundation.

Traditional Christmas concert of Centro Scuola e Cultura Italiana. The Schola Cantorum children's choir was directed by Franca Di Giovanni, at the George Weston Recital Hall, in The Toronto Centre for the Performing Arts.

Toronto, 1977: Umberto Eco presents The Name of the Rose *in Canada, with Giancarlo Boccotti, Director of the Istituto Italiano di Cultura, and Alberto Di Giovanni, President of the Dante Alighieri Society of Toronto.*

Roberto Benigni after his Lectura Dantis with Alberto, Caroline and Annamaria Di Giovanni.

The Honourable Romeo Ricciuti, Governor of the Region of Abruzzo and later Italy's Secretary of Agriculture, congratulates Caroline Morgan Di Giovanni, Chair of the Metropolitan Separate School Board (Toronto Catholic District School Board).

A group of Italian-Canadian students in the semester program in Italy pose with their parents in front of the Coliseum during a visit to Rome.

The Italians of Toronto celebrating Italy's World Cup win in Spain (1982) with the participation of 500,000 people, according to official sources. It was the largest spontaneous gathering in the history of Canada.

On the occasion of the 125th anniversary of the founding of Canada, members of the Italian Canadian community in Toronto were awarded the Gold Medal of Honor for Merit by the Government of Canada. Included in the picture: Paul Ariemma, Mary Bartolini, Father Gianni Carparelli, Brent Chambers, Antonietta Ciccarelli, Steve Corvese, Manlio D'Ambrosio, Caroline Di Giovanni (representing husband Alberto Di Giovanni), Carmine Di Paola, Helen Lettieri, Maria Minna, Julius A. Molinaro, Fosca Montagnese, Lorenzo Petricone, Joseph Piccininni, Fortunato Rao, Assunta Scaife, Maria Sgro, Joseph Sorbara (representing his father Sam Sorbara), Lisa Stefanini (representing her father Giancarlo Stefanini), Michael Tibollo and Michael Yealand. Absent: Isa Scotti. (October 1992)

EIGHT

Economic Success and Social Awareness

I THINK I CAN SAY with reasonable certainty that the cleverest portrayal of the profile currently enjoyed by Italian Canadians was captured in the headline in the *Toronto Star*, in May 24, 1999, which introduced an extensive article on the front page, about the Italian community: *"It's chic to be Italian in the GTA."* That expression captured the Anglo-Saxon attitude, summed up by the subtitle *"community holds dual identities,"* as well as with the heading used on the inside pages: *"Italians feel at home in the GTA."* That same press report disclosed the results of a survey on a significant sample of the population of Toronto. The question put to a representative sample of the Italian community was: "To what group do people primarily identify themselves?" According to the author of the article, Donovan Vincent, the results of the survey had a surprising outcome: 73% replied "Canadian," 58% "Torontonian," 49% "Italian," 49% "local" and 46% "religious." Asked to comment on that outcome, I replied: "That's not strange, because it indicates a high level of integration, yet strong ties to culture. It's not a contradiction."

Although Italians had been immigrating to Canada since the second half of the nineteenth century, it is notably in the decade of 1955-65

71

that the massive wave of emigration from Italy poured an unskilled work force into construction firms, railway building, manufacturing and food farming. After half a century, the Italian Canadian workforce looks very different, as seen in their main activities: 12% are managers, 21% professionals, technicians and traders, 18% are administrative employees, and 19% skilled workers. As far as birth registry, 66% of them were born in Canada, while 87% of those who had immigrated before 1966 had acquired Canadian citizenship.

For the report in the *Toronto Star*, I explained the new configuration of the status of citizenship for Italians as being "... *largely due to the federal multiculturalism policy introduced in 1971 by Prime Minister Trudeau, an event which was a "turning point" for the community because it fostered a feeling of acceptance. I helped set up citizenship courts in schools and neighbourhoods for the tens of thousands of Italian-born people who happily pledged a citizenship oath to Canada. We did this because we felt citizenship is important. Many then felt obliged to participate in Canada's institutions and political system, especially voting.*"

In respect to economic success, long gone are the days when Italians were called "ditch-digger," "spaghetti-bender" or "wop. By the end of the sixties, well-being and economic fortunes had seen steady and progressive growth. The result was a new self-awareness, which has matured for the Italian Canadians into a desire to step up the social ladder and also a willingness to participate in public life. At present, there is no place in the industrial and financial arenas, nor in the political and cultural life, in which the Italians do not play leading roles, often significantly profitable.

As the community became increasingly more mature and well-developed, there was readiness to take on a leadership role in every area of life whether it be social, labour related, economic, political and so on. In this context it is necessary to mention the contribution of the Italian-Canadian women. The first who must be mentioned is Isa Scotti. She was born in Bari in 1920, and eventually, in Naples, she met the man who would become her husband, the brilliant Milanese journalist, Arturo Scotti. Together with her husband and their daughters, Susanna and Rosanna, they arrived in Canada in 1952. Arturo Scotti along with Dan Iannuzzi had founded the *Corriere Canadese*, but only two years after his arrival he died prematurely. Isa Scotti became director of the Italian Immigrant Aid Society, a non-profit organization to support and guide newcomers from Italy. The association, founded in 1950 at the first Catholic church for Italians, which today is St. Patrick's Church, played a major role for the benefit of the Italians right up until the end of the sixties, when it was decided it would join COSTI.

Isa Scotti dedicated herself to social assistance activities but, aware of her skills and abilities, also wished to become a strong voice, determined and vigorous, for the sake of those she helped, getting them used to being considered a community entity and training them to know how to self-manage. She was later appointed a citizenship judge. It was no accident that a personality like that became a forerunner of the Italian-Canadian women's movement that in 1975, The International Year of the Woman, would contribute to a profound transformation of the community, encouraging women of Italian origin to meet success never previously imagined. The Scotti daughters, Susanna and Rosanna, having already distinguished themselves during their university years, were among the first women named to executive positions in the civil service. One of their peers, Raffaella Di Pasquale Di Cecco, also distinguished herself in government service, as an Officer in the Ontario Ministry of Education and in particular, as the Executive Director of the (Ontario) Royal Commission on Learning, tabled in 1994.

An individual who was long and consistently among the leaders of community life is Maria Grifone. Born in 1945 in Molise, Maria arrived in Canada at the age of thirteen. Towards the end of the sixties, she took part in the Company of Young Canadians, where she met Roberto Bandiera, whom she married in 1970. Together they shared more than half a century of artistic endeavours in the community. One particular episode of their lives left a lasting impression on many of us. At that time, it was popular in the warm Toronto summer to enjoy the Italian-style picnic, held alternatively by CHIN and the *Corriere Canadese* on one of the Toronto islands. It was at the picnic held in 1970, sponsored by the *Corriere Canadese*, that Maria and Roberto, along with a few colleagues, were protagonists of a remarkable presentation of a pantomime of which I will speak in Chap. 13. Throughout the years Maria and Roberto engaged in various ways in the social and cultural scenes and associations of both the regions of Molise and Sicily. Sadly, Maria passed away suddenly in 2014.

Meanwhile, the 19-year-old Giovanna Tozzi from Agropoli, would arrive in 1973 and by 1985 would become chief editor of the weekly newspaper *Lo Specchio*. In 1979 Tozzi had created "Donna" (Woman), a unique forum for the development of the role of women in Canadian society. Publication ceased in 2004, a loss to the community.

The year 1975 was marked very incisively by the celebration of the International Year of the Woman. A slow but unstoppable movement began to free the women of the world from the many constraints that hinder them from full self-realization in various social contexts. Among those who strongly committed themselves to translate into reality the principles set out in the Year of the Woman was Angela Nadin, married Piscitelli, who had a brilliant career in the field of education as a secondary school principal. She dedicated herself to community activities to which she made a remarkable contribution. Another woman who has risen to prominent roles within the Italian-Canadian community is Maria Augimeri, who graduated in anthropology at York University and then after her marriage to Odoardo Di Santo, embraced a life of politics at the municipal level. She served as Councillor in the Municipality of North York and then on the Metropolitan Toronto Council. After the amalgamation of the City of Toronto, Maria was repeatedly re-elected, serving the community for over 30 consecutive years.

In recalling a few examples of women who have made an outstanding contribution to transforming and modernizing the Canadian community, how can I possibly omit mentioning Caroline Morgan, just because she is my wife? During a TV program, journalist Angelo Persichilli came to define her as "a naturalized Italian-Canadian." An American from Philadelphia and from distant Irish and French ancestry, Caroline was instrumental in the years of the great transformation of the Catholic school system in Toronto. In 1987, she was the first woman elected as Chairman of the Metropolitan Separate School Board, now known as the Toronto Catholic District School Board. Considering the prevailing mindset within the Canadian Catholic world, that was in itself quite revolutionary. But the real breakthrough came soon after, when Caroline carved unprecedented change into the conduct of school business: parents' participation in decision making, teaching reforms, the appointment of lay women principals, inclusion of women in leadership roles in general, giving the school system the opportunity for interaction with the different language groups and, thanks to her report "Anti-Racism and Ethnic Relations Policy," the introduction of the teaching of several languages in curricular courses. Edward Nelligan, Director of Education of the MSSB, called her "the best ever member of this Board." In the years after her chairmanship, Caroline was able to distinguish herself as well for the reports she presented at various conferences in North America, and the publication of several essays on the philosophy of Catholic education. She was also elected as a councillor for Metropolitan Toronto, presiding over the sensitive special committee, "Metro Task Force on Services for Young Children and Families."

The widespread acquisition of familiarity with English and the Canadian "way of life" has removed insecurity from the Italian psyche and distrust from the Anglo-Saxon. The fact that the *Corriere Canadese* has become a bilingual publication in which articles written in English share space with the texts in Italian, bears an obvious significance. In 1999, the *Toronto Star* pointed out that Italian style is now "cool," thanks to a general falling in love with the art, cuisine and lifestyle of Italy, as well as for the big names in fashion such as Gucci, Versace and many more. For its part, the *Corriere Canadese*, in an article on February 2, 2003, also wondered if the Italians might consider themselves a "founding" people in addition to the British and French. It argued that:

> *The answer can be found in the awareness displayed by Italian-Canadians living in Canada. All of them – those who left Italy because of their needs, those who were born here, and those who*

have arrived now to put their abilities to the test – live in this country as protagonists.

The numbers clearly indicate the consequence, even quantitatively, of the Italian Canadians, present virtually everywhere in the vast territory lying between the Atlantic and the Pacific, and heavily concentrated in the major cities: more than 500,000 in Toronto, more than 300,000 in Montreal, more than 100,000 in Vancouver.

One often hears: "It is the Italians who built Toronto." Obviously, this is hyperbole. However, it is certainly true that the Italians have contributed in an extraordinary way to building Toronto. A popular saying that went the rounds years ago held that Italian immigrants after the war came here with the idea of finding a country where the streets were paved with gold, but discovered instead that the roads were not only not gold plated but often were not paved at all, and therefore it was up to them to lay the asphalt. The construction industry, in fact, was the first and most important area in which Italian immigrants found employment opportunities, and then also business ones. From the mass of hundreds of thousands of immigrant workers, in fact, emerged a group of enterprising leaders, founders of construction and development companies.

For decades, the main construction projects involved roads, railways, bridges, viaducts, and only rarely, some buildings, because almost all the houses were made of wood. Then, after the Second World War, a spectacular construction boom took place, which leapt forward with the construction of large commercial and residential skyscrapers. Among the first to stand out in this area was Nick Di Lorenzo who hailed from Torre dei Passeri in Abruzzo. He revolutionized certain methods of construction by introducing a process of prefabrication that brought him resounding success. Elvio Del Zotto, a lawyer of Friulian background, was a major player in the creation of the Ontario Foundation of the National Congress of Italian Canadians, and a founding member of the Italian Canadian Benevolent Corporation. His father Jack was an Italian stonemason who came to Canada in 1927, worked in the mines near Timmins, and eventually started a home building firm in Toronto. Elvio, together with his brothers Angelo and Leo, took over the company founded by their father and built it into Tridel Corp., a major real estate developer based in Toronto. Casa Del Zotto is one of the high rise apartment towers built for seniors on the same campus as Villa Colombo and the Columbus Centre. A generous and enthusiastic supporter of the arts, Elvio Del Zotto was the first major contributor to the creation of Centro Scuola e Cultura Italiana.

There now are many successful Italian immigrants who have found fortune in the construction industry. By the nineties, the story of the streets of gold was supplanted by a remark attributed to Prime Minister Brian Mulroney who said: "Italian parents have built the great skyscrapers; today, it's their children who own them." Great success stories almost always have behind them individuals of exceptional talent. Two examples are Rudy Bratty and John Cutruzzola. Rudy Bratty, the son of carpenter who emigrated from Friuli in 1922, is today a legend in Canadian building. Always generously present in grand socio-cultural initiatives of the community, he has built thousands of buildings and created entire neighbourhoods in the Greater Toronto Area, focusing on the highest quality and aesthetic harmony with the natural environment. John Cutruzzola is the Calabrese contractor who literally transformed mud into diamonds. Yorkville was a heap of aging shacks, warehouses and small factories, crumbling and abandoned, that an investor found himself owning without knowing what he might do with it all. Cutruzzola was given carte blanche and the availability of a bevy of architects. He decided not to demolish even a small wall, but to render precious every detail of that remarkable and famous neighbourhood. It was he who would indicate what and how things should be done. Today, Yorkville is an icon of luxury and one of the major attractions of Toronto.

It should be noted, however, that the captains of industry of Italian origin were not limited to the field of the construction only but embraced the most varied industries, from food to insurance, trade, finance, and so on, up to the highest levels. In this regard, I propose several examples, to allow a clearer understanding of their diversity.

I start with Sam Ciccolini, who, not coincidentally, is affectionately nicknamed "parsley." As this tasty seasoning functions in the kitchen, so Ciccolini is fine and works well in any context. He was born in Italy, grew up and studied in Toronto and looks back on nearly 40 years of commitment to the business world, in the field of insurance and various commercial and industrial sectors. Sam is a true personification of philanthropy. He is one of the protagonists of the multiple beneficial achievements of Villa Charities, being actively involved and supporting a bit of everything, from child care centres to hospitals and sports, including football and hockey.

Another example that I want to introduce is that of Fausto Gaudio, founder and president of a banking institution from the1990s, the Italian Canadian Savings. Gaudio, who holds a university degree in economics, works in finance, a volatile field, and one in which he has entered with alacrity. For his part he considers sharing professional achievements essential, as he confirms in a statement about the donations made by the Italian Canadian Savings: "Donations reflect our corporate commitment, not only to our members but for the entire community in which we work and where we are and wish to be an active part of the social and economic progress."

Another significant enterprise, St. Joseph Communications, was started by Gaetano Gagliano, an immigrant from Sicily who arrived in the 1950s and worked first on the railroad. Then, in Toronto, he opened a small printing business, taking care of his family of 10 children. The business grew very rapidly, into one of the biggest enterprises in Canada, a real media empire that includes magazines and television, among its varied branches. One of his sons, Tony Gagliano, took on the executive role when his father retired.

I'd like to add three other personalities active in the community in the past 40 years. Rocco Lofranco, from Pisticci, Lucania, came to Canada as a hairdresser. He became very involved with the National Congress of Italian Canadians and with Villa Charities; he was a radio host with CHIN; and an activist with the Progressive Conservative Party. He was a friend of the Hon. William Davis, Premier of Ontario from 1971 to

1985, one of the most highly regarded politicians in Canada. In 1974, Rocco Lofranco accompanied Premier Davis on a famous trip to Italy, and was able to open a channel of communication between the Italian community and the provincial government of the time. He has also been instrumental in promoting the sport of soccer, serving as president of the Toronto Italia S.C., and of the National Soccer League.

Two more Friulani deserving of mention are Primo Di Luca and Fred Zorzi. Primo Di Luca has been active with the National Congress of Italian Canadians as well as Villa Charities. Most of all, he is known for his outstanding leadership with the well-organized Famee Furlane. He spearheaded the fundraising drive for the reconstruction of Friuli after the earthquake of 1976. Di Luca distinguished himself for the excellent management of the vast rebuilding project in the region. Today he is the Honorary Consul of Canada in Friuli. He has helped to develop a thriving commercial link between his region and Ontario. As well, he was instrumental in creating the Famee Furlane club and senior citizens residences in the G.T.A. The second name I wish to recall with great affection is Fred Zorzi, a brilliant law partner of Elvio Del Zotto, and an outspoken champion of the Italian National Congress. He gained admiration for his professional integrity, giving many of us high hopes for his leadership. He took part in the unforgettable first encounter of the Italian Canadian community with Prime Minister Pierre Elliott Trudeau. Zorzi addressed Trudeau with impeccable style, saying without hesitation: "The time has finally come to recognize with concrete action the Italian contribution to the building of the Canadian nation, and support the linguistic rights of minorities." It was a moment of strong ethnic and moral substance which marked an historic passage for the Italian Canadians. Fred Zorzi passed away at a young age, before he could fulfil his potential.

Mention must be made of the dynamic career of Sergio Marchionne, who hails from Chieti, Abruzzo, where his father was an officer of the Carabinieri. The family moved to Canada when he was 12 years old. He attended St. Michael's College School, then obtained university degrees in business and in law. He maintained a close connection with the

Toronto Italian community while rising through the ranks of international finance. This took him first to Switzerland, then to Torino where he became head of the iconic Fiat company. He is widely recognized for his bold step of combining Fiat with the Detroit-based Chrysler brand. His latest move was to become the chief executive of Ferrari.

Finally, here's something particularly unique, combining entrepreneurial and cultural creativity. In this category we find Roberto and Lucia Martella, owners for half a century of *grano* (with the lowercase g) Restaurant on Yonge Street. *grano* is one of the most innovative places in Toronto. The *Globe and Mail* defines it as: "… *a piazza where people come together to eat, meet and debate*." The family originally emigrated after the Second World War, from Atri, in Abruzzo. The Martellas turned their restaurant into a place that not only serves good pasta, but also mixes socializing with ideas, where conferences are held, and all kinds of special events and initiatives take place.

NINE

The Rise to Political Power

Even after being freed from the stigma of being marginalized, considered only as the labour force, even after being fully accepted in a community context, for Canadian Anglophones, the Italians remained a separate entity. On the social level they were considered "picnic folk," that is, congenial, likeable people with whom one could socialize pleasantly, sit with amiably around the dining table, spend time with delightfully at the café or on the golf course, and happily party with in the parlour or in the garden. "Picnic folk" – in short, pleasant companions, hugs and kisses, but nothing more. Of course, worthy of the utmost respect for their valued contribution as business owners, executives, artists, technicians, intellectuals and even employees and workers, having a sincere willingness to do business and have you do business with them. "Picnic folk" all the same, meaning that Italians could certainly not be recognized for having the aptitude to function in a matter so serious, in the Commonwealth tradition, the most respected and respectable of duties, and that is the administration of public affairs.

There is an episode that demonstrates how the stereotype of "picnic folk" was rooted in the Canadian image of the Italians, even after decades of an Italian Canadian presence at the most senior levels of government, both local and federal. In the nineties, during one of his trips to Italy, Jean Chretien, one of the most popular of Canadian prime ministers, having decided to visit L'Aquila, wanted the meeting with the representatives of institutions and businesses to take place at a picnic in one of the beautiful parks in the city. My proposal to include an artistic interlude was supported by MP Sergio Marchi, who was also on the trip. However, the Prime Minister's staff reacted with somewhat arrogant rudeness. Actually, Mr. Chretien's request was not an attitude of condescension toward Italians. On the contrary, it was the old stereotype that the "picnic" was the best way to demonstrate one's friendly disposition.

If up to 1971 the presence of Italian Canadians in the political life was scarce, the implementation of the policy of multiculturalism invited much greater participation by Italian Canadians as candidates for office at the municipal, provincial, and federal levels of government.

I have already mentioned Carletto Caccia, who served first on Toronto City Council from 1966 to 1968, and was then elected as a Member of Parliament, in 1968. He served on the Trudeau Cabinet as Minister of Labour, and then as Minister of the Environment. Consistently re-elected for three decades, he only retired from politics in 2000, when in-fighting in the riding resulted in his departure. During that same period, a number of other Italian Canadians have distinguished themselves in public life, representing the community in the cities, the province, and in Ottawa.

The Canadian confederation is governed by the Federal Parliament at the national level, and Provincial legislatures for the ten provinces and the three Territories. They have well-defined jurisdictions, and legislative powers. Members are elected when elections are called, according to parliamentary democracy. At the Federal level there is also a Senate, whose members are appointed, generally by the majority party in power. At the local level, municipal councillors are concerned with the city services and bylaws, while school trustees oversee the Boards of Education, responsible for the administration of the systems as a whole. Both of these bodies are elected for fixed terms of office. The election of Italian Canadians to represent their local communities at the municipal level has been relatively common through the years, with participation steadily increasing. For this reason, it will be impractical to name the many Italian Canadians who have played important roles in the daily routines of families and children.

The greater challenge came from entry in political office at the Federal or the Provincial level. The first two members from the post-war Italian Canadians were Dante De Monte, for the Ontario legislature, and Carletto (Charles) Caccia, at the Federal level. Both were members of the Liberal Party. Dante De Monte served at Queen's Park, the Ontario legislature, from 1967 to 1971. He was a lawyer, known as a perfect gentleman, and already active in his university days. He was the first president of the Italian Club at the University of Toronto. Of Friulani descent, he remained active in the Friuliani community in Toronto. Following Carletto Caccia, the number of Italian Canadians in Parliament in Ottawa increased by many members, all within the ranks of the Liberal Party. The MPs and their terms of office include: Ursula Appolloni (1974, '79, '80), Sergio Marchi (1984, '88, '93, '97), John Nunziata (1984, '88, '93, and as an Independent, '97), Maurizio Bevilaqua (1988, '90, '93, '97, 2000, '04, '06, '08), Joe Volpe (1988, '93, '97, 2000, '04, '06, '08), Maria Minna (1993, '97, 2000, '04, 06, '08), Tony Ianno (1993, '97, '2000, '04), Albina Guarnieri (1997, 2000, '04, '06, '08), Judy Sgro (by-election 1999, 2000, '04, '06, '08, '11). For the Conservative Party: Paul Calandra (2008, '11), Julian Fantino (by-election 2010, '11).

The Italian Canadians who have been appointed as Cabinet Ministers in various portfolios over the years include: Caccia, Bevilaqua, Marchi, Minna, Volpe, Sgro, and Fantino.

The most successful politician from the Italian Canadian community has been Sergio Marchi, from a riding in the Toronto area. Born in Buenos Aires, Argentina, in 1956, his family of Friuli origin moved to Toronto, when he was a young child. He obtained a degree in Urban Studies and Sociology from York University in 1979. By 1982, at the age of 26, he was elected Alderman in the city of North York, a district later amalgamated into Toronto. In 1984, he was elected as a Liberal Member of Parliament, and appointed to Cabinet as Minister of Citizenship and Immigration, then Minister of the Environment, and finally, Minister of International Trade. During the Chretien era he was the Ontario lieutenant for the Prime Minister. In 1999 he resigned his seat in order to accept an appointment as the Canadian Ambassador to the World Trade Centre in Geneva, Switzerland.

To replace Sergio Marchi in the Cabinet, Prime Minister Chretien appointed the young Maurizio Bevilaqua. Originally from Sulmona, Abruzzo, Bevilaqua was first elected to Parliament when he was just 28 years old. His Cabinet post was as Minister responsible for Science, Research, and Development. In 2008, amidst general incredulity, he resigned his seat in order to run for the office of Mayor of the City of Vaughan, a position he won handily. In his place, Julian Fantino won the by-election for the Conservative Party. A career police officer, Fantino had served as Chief of the police services in London, Ontario, and in York Region, and in Metropolitan Toronto. He also served as head of the Ontario Provincial Police before running for political office. In Ottawa, he was welcomed by Prime Minister Harper, and named to a Cabinet position.

Another MP with a strong presence in the Italian Canadian community was Joe Volpe, for the Liberal Party. Hailing from Monteleone, Puglia, Volpe was a teacher and a Vice Principal with the Toronto Catholic District School Board before going to Ottawa. Within the Liberal Party caucus there, he took part in an outspoken group of members who were pressing for change. He became Minister of Citizenship and Immigration in the short-lived government led by Prime Minister Paul Martin.

The success of Italian Canadians in the Federal government can be regarded with some satisfaction, while at the Ontario Provincial level community members achieved even greater prominence. In two cases our members came close to the top of the Liberal party, as leader and Premier. I refer to Greg Sorbara and Sandra Pupatello.

For the New Democratic Party, the Provincial election of 1975 saw the somewhat unexpected election of three Italian Canadians: Odoardo

Di Santo, Tony Grande, and Tony Lupusella. All three had been community activists in the past; one man, Odoardo Di Santo, seemed to have politics in his DNA. The three members all continued to participate in the community, enhancing the level of debate with their input. The Liberals soon understood that a fair portion of their electorate had been drawn to the other party, so they immediately took positive steps to attract Italian Canadian candidates. This action achieved partial success, on the third attempt, with the election of Michael Spensieri. Meanwhile, the three NDPers were re-elected in 1977 and again in 1981. Only in 1985 did the Liberals succeed in regaining popularity in the Italian Canadian community, with the election of Joseph Cordiano, Claudio Polsinelli, and Greg Sorbara. The latter surged upwards as a star in the Liberal party. In 1986, Antonio Lupusella changed his party affiliation from the NDP to the Liberal. In the election of 1987, two more members joined the Liberal caucus at Queen's Park, namely Laureano Leone and Gino Martrandola. This election resulted in the first Liberal party minority government in half a century, upsetting the long-standing Conservative hegemony.

However, the Liberal experience under Premier David Peterson proved short-lived. Under the leadership of Bob Rae, the New Democratic Party swept to a resounding majority, and he became the Premier. Although two Italian Canadians had been Cabinet Ministers under Peterson, the disillusioned electorate punished them with defeat. Only Sorbara and Cordiano won re-election. For the first time in Ontario, the social democrats of the NDP formed the government. The 1990 election brought to the government benches Antony Peruzza, Rosario Marchese, Tony Silipo, Tony Rizzo, and Giorgio Mammoliti. The Italian Canadians took part in the Cabinet first with Rosario Marchese, Minister of Culture, then with the appointment of Tony Silipo, a former Chair of the Toronto Board of Education, as Minister of Education.

Five years later the Conservatives were back in power, under Mike Harris, a right wing ideologue. Silipo and Marchese were re-elected for the diminished NDP, while Anna Marie Castrilli won a seat for the Liberals. A lawyer, and past-president of the National Congress of

Italian Canadians, Ms Castrilli had also been a distinguished Chair of the Governing Council of the University of Toronto. Also elected for the Liberals was Mike Colle, who had been a member of the Metropolitan Toronto Council, and Chair of the Toronto Transit Commission. Another Italian Canadian Liberal elected for the first time was Sandra Pupatello, from Windsor, a dynamic MPP who would rise to the top of the Liberal establishment. Mario Sergio was elected for the Liberals, defeating the NDP Giorgio Mammoliti. Joseph Cordiano was re-elected, but Greg Sorbara chose not to run again. His seat was captured by the popular Al Palladini, who ran for the Conservatives. He was immediately named to Cabinet.

At this point the Liberals began the search for a new leader. Both Joseph Cordiano and Annamarie Castrilli presented themselves to the convention floor. Greg Sorbara had run for this position at the previous party convention, but he had come in third place. This time Cordiano came in third, while the attempt by Castrilli appeared to be premature. Her loss seemed to mark the end of what might have been a brilliant political career. In the next election she was a candidate for the Conservatives, but she failed to win the seat.

Premier Mike Harris triumphed again in the 1999 Ontario election. Al Palladini held the prestigious Cabinet position of Minister of International Commerce. The newly-elected Tina Molinari was given a junior Cabinet post as Minister without Portfolio. Among the Italian Canadian candidates for the Liberals, the re-elected members were: Colle, Cordiano, Sergio, and Pupatello, while Marchese was the only NDP member re-elected. During the term, Minister Al Palladini died suddenly from a heart attack. For the by-election to fill the vacancy, Greg Sorbara returned triumphantly, ready to climb the political ladder again.

In 2003, the Liberals led by Dalton McGuinty won an election majority. Then Premier McGuinty selected Greg Sorbara as his "right hand man," giving him the role of Minister of Finance, the second highest position in the Cabinet. Sorbara was also serving as the President of the Liberal Party, at the same time. Other Italian Canadians elected this time were: Mike Colle, Lorenzo Berardinetti, Joseph Cordiano, Sandra Pupatello, Mario Racco, and Mario Sergio. The only Italian Canadian re-elected for the NDP was Rosario Marchese. This time the Cabinet represented a larger number of Italian Canadian Ministers; joining Greg Sorbara were Joseph Cordiano, Sandra Pupatello, and Mike Colle.

During this term the electorate of Ontario would witness a number of surprises. First and foremost was the resignation of Finance Minister Greg Sorbara. He stepped aside in the course of a judicial inquiry, but ultimately he was fully exonerated. Then there was another parliamentary controversy in which Mike Colle became the scapegoat. Joseph Cordiano became intolerant of the backroom intrigues, and decided to abandon the political life. The Liberals would receive a new mandate under Premier McGuinty in the election of 2007. The Italian Canadians elected this time included Mike Colle, Sandra Pupatello, Lorenzo Berardinetti, Mario Sergio, a returning Greg Sorbara, and for the first time, the television journalist Laura Albanese. For the NDP, Rosario Marchese won his seat; by now he had become a senior member of the NDP caucus. In the Liberal Cabinet, however, only Sandra Pupatello represented the Italian Canadian group of members.

This takes us to the lacklustre election of 2011, notable for voter indifference and low turnouts across Ontario. Pupatello did not seek re-election. Premier McGuinty returned with a minority government situation, with Sorbara, Sergio, Colle and Albanese re-elected. Marchese returned, often acting as the Italian-speaking spokesperson for the NDP. This was the moment for another bombshell from Greg Sorbara. He announced his final retirement from political life, in order to spend more time with his family. The by-election to fill the vacancy was won by the Liberal Stephen De Luca, a union activist. The riding north of Toronto had increased in population due to new housing developments, very popular with Italian Canadian families.

The surprises were not over yet. Now it was Premier McGuinty who, in the midst of controversy, resigned as Leader and announced his departure from the Legislature. Sandra Pupatello stepped up as a strong contender to succeed him. A winner in the opinion polls, she was leading at the convention right up to the final ballot, which she lost by a handful of votes to Kathleen Wynne. Pupatello took the unexpected defeat with dignity, extending a gracious gesture of solidarity with the new Premier, the first woman to hold that post in Ontario.

In the subsequent, swiftly-called election of 2014, Kathleen Wynne emerged with a large Liberal majority. Rosario Marchese was defeated by a Liberal newcomer from the Chinese community in that downtown riding. The returning Italian Canadian Liberals included Mike Colle, Lorenzo Berardinetti, Laura Albanese, Mario Sergio, named a Minister without Portfolio for Senior Citizens, and Stephen De Luca, named Minister of Transportation. This consistent presence of Italian Canadians in public office guarantees even greater participation in the next generation.

TEN

Appointments to National Institutions

ONE INDICATION OF THE SUCCESS of Italian Canadians in public life is shown by the number of appointments to high office at the national level. In Canada the Senate, known as the Red Chamber, has traditionally been regarded with esteem. For a modern, democratic state, however, there are some contradictions. First of all, members are not elected but are appointed to this law-making body by the government of the day. This means that the selections fall, inevitably, to individuals who have proven their loyalty to their political party. Furthermore the Senate, notwithstanding its prestige, is generally regarded as obsolete. Many people would like to see it reformed, or eliminated altogether. Most recently, the Senate has been a theatre of great controversy, yet it continues to operate as usual.

The current ambiguities, however, should not diminish the value of the Italian Canadians who have been appointed to the Senate thus far. The first to be named was Pietro Rizzuto, a Montrealer, chosen by Prime Minister Trudeau, in 1976. One year later, Trudeau selected Peter Bosa, a former Councillor from the City of York (later Toronto), and a pillar of the well-organized and dynamic Friuliani community. This appointment was welcomed by all because he was recognized as a man of absolute integrity, with a gift for productive dialogue.

In 1990, the Conservative Prime Minister Brian Mulroney appointed Consiglio Di Nino, a former banker. This was also a popular choice, representing as it did the generation of Italian Canadians who had arrived in the country as children, and grown up more in Canada than in Italy. Di Nino was noted first as President of the Canadian Italian Business and Professional Association, and then as President of Villa Charities, the umbrella organization for Villa Colombo and the Columbus Centre. As Peter Bosa had done when an earthquake struck Friuli, in 1976, Senator Di Nino headed the committee to raise funds to assist the city of l'Aquila, in Abruzzo, when an earthquake struck in 2009. Other committee members with roots in the region included Pal Di Iulio, Director of Villa Charities, and myself.

The Senate is the second house of Parliament, considered the place for "sober second thoughts" for lawmakers. Also in Ottawa, operating independently from the government, the nine judges of the Supreme Court preside over final decisions in judicial matters. Here, too, Italian Canadians have been proudly represented by an outstanding lawyer, Dean of the University of Toronto Law School, Frank Iacobucci. His appointment also came from Conservative Prime Minister Brian Mulroney, in 1991. He served in this demanding position until 2005, when he retired as a judge. Since then he has accepted several positions related to First Nations issues, such as the Chair of the selection committee for members of the Indian Residential Schools Truth and Reconciliation Commission; an inquiry into the presence of First Nations people on juries; and in 2013, as the Ontario lead negotiator in the First Nations Ring of Fire process.

An important breakthrough for Italian Canadians in Ontario was the 1979 appointment of lawyer Lorenzo De Cecco as a Provincial Court Judge. This first such nomination came from the well-liked and respected Conservative Premier William Davis. De Cecco served in this capacity until 1989. His appointment opened the way for the next judicial appointee, Salvatore Merenda, a lawyer who had been a popular and innovative President of the National Congress of Italian Canadians. In addition to judicial appointments, two major law enforcement organizations have seen Italian Canadians at the top. Giuliano Zaccardelli served an honourable term as the head of the Royal Canadian Mounted Police, the famous RCMP. I have already mentioned Julian Fantino, Chief of Police in three different jurisdictions, and then head of the Ontario Provincial Police, before running for election as a Member of Parliament.

Such high-ranking officials in these fields have broken down the stereotypes that inhibit full participation in Canadian institutions. Still, there are no roses without thorns. A patronage system can easily develop within a community, at a lower level, that depends more on favouritism than deserving merit. This is true for any community group, and applies to both the Liberal and the Conservative political parties. C'est la vie.

ELEVEN

The Catholic Church and Italian Canadians

THE ITALIANS WHO CAME to Canada in the fifties and sixties in increasing numbers met a socio-cultural and linguistically different scene from the one left behind in Italy, but perhaps no one could have imagined that this contrast would also affect the way they would practice their own religious faith. For all its universal values, the Catholic Church in Canada was organized both structurally and pastorally in a very different way from the Italian one. I am not referring simply to the influence, often decisive, that the Catholic Church has had in the history and ongoing reality of Italy. The religious and spiritual substance is obviously the same here, but the pastoral differences in customs and practices of everyday occurrences in the lives of hundreds of thousands of Italians in Canada, either newcomers or those born here, are significantly different from parish practice in Italy.

Back in the heroic years of the great influx of immigrants, the Church had obviously been a point of reference of the utmost importance to the disinherited masses who suffered from disorientation and difficulty integrating into a society not only very different from the one of their origin but also often hostile. Early in the 20th century, when the first wave of immigrants clustered in the area known as the Ward, the parish of Our Lady of Mount Carmel, at Dundas and St. Patrick St., organized a Mutual Aid Society for them. Then, in the immediate aftermath of WWII, the parishes of St. Francis Church, near College St. and St. Agnes, in the Grace and Dundas St. area, made their church basements available as the meeting place for families to be .reunited upon the arrival of newcomers. Despite numerous obstacles, the Church took care of welfare projects designed to mitigate the fundamental hardships, and above all, sooth the afflictions of everyday life, offering the comfort of devotional practices and the loving atmosphere inspired by the hope of happiness in the afterlife, and the gift of words that were morally uplifting.

With the passage of time, however, and as improvements advanced in both the economic conditions and the social status of Italian immigrants, all this lost its importance. In Canada, religion hasn't functioned as a means of identity for the Italian Canadians so much as a connotation of the motherland. It has largely been watered down from a deep-rooted conviction of conscience to a sort of affectionate tradition. The external aspect largely prevails over the interior one: Sunday mass, baptisms, weddings, funerals, major holidays such as Christmas or Easter, and the feast of the patron saints of villages and towns of origin of the ancestors are occasions much revered and honoured with widespread participation. But the sincere emotion that is put forth is related more to ceremonial and social decorum than with any intimate spiritual outpouring. It is somehow the same phenomenon that underlies the generosity with which so many Italian Canadians have helped to fund the construction of many of the Catholic places of worship built in the Greater Toronto Area.

The reasons for the picture I have briefly described are numerous and complex, rooted in the particular context of the Canadian system, in which religious organizations of all faiths cannot take advantage of government subsidies nor have the opportunity to influence the management of public affairs and the choice of those who are appointed to public office. It seems that here a man of the cloth, both in the parish and at the hierarchical level, often acts more as a manager than a pastor. He must take care of all tasks, whether they be logistical, administrative, or priestly; he must raise the money necessary for himself and for the services for the parishioners, as well as contributing to the general operation of the diocese.

The first priests who came from Italy to minister to the immigrants suffered much the same disorientation as the typical immigrant. They had not been taught how to be managers. Often, struggling to deal with the daily pastoral duties, bewildered and oppressed as they were by the unusual load of managerial responsibilities, they ended up with poor outcomes as priests and administrators. Obviously, day after day, they had to learn. The future seminarians who were born in Canada have benefited from their familiarity with Canadian life; they are "born learned," as they say. To be a priest in such a way implies a cultural and pragmatic relationship with the church community which is quite different from the usual standard in Italy. Not infrequently, anger and misunderstandings arose and, above all, a detachment from the real problems of the community that kept the church for the most part alien to the socio-cultural dynamics and the tensions in the workplace. This was certainly the result of the general attitude of the hierarchy, which was not very responsive to the guidelines set forth by the social doctrine of the Church.

The great ecumenical fervour communicated in the sixties by the Second Vatican Council did not propel the Canadian Church towards progress but, on the contrary, was used as an opportunity to strengthen the authority of the church hierarchy over the faithful, creating a growing gap between these and their pastors. Marriage preparation is an eloquent indicator of this regression. In a multi-ethnic society such as Canada, it has been quite common for young people from diverse cultural and family backgrounds to marry. Moreover, the makeup of families which join Catholicism with Judaism or with Protestantism is one of the resources in which are rooted the vibrancy and the creativity of a peaceful Canadian social syncretism. However, mixed marriages of young Catholics often encounter many complicated, even insurmountable obstacles, that obviously do not discourage these kinds of relationships but rather lead to alienation from the Church and an increase in civil marriages and common law unions.

Many of the priests assigned to the Italian Canadian community gave it their all to be appointed pastors and thus gain important administrative powers as well as a presumed legitimacy to perpetuate in Canada the Italian tradition of guidance and control over the community. They distinguished themselves very little, however, in the struggles alongside the workers for the sake of the cultural and social progress of the community. Among the outstanding exceptions, Fr. Orestes Cerbara and Fr. Nicola De Angelis deserve special recognition and enduring gratitude. The former, hailing from Colleferro, province of Frosinone, was educated in Italy and the United States, was perfectly bilingual, and was the first President of the Italian Pastoral Ministry of Toronto. Cerbara was an active participant in the developing strength within the community. In the field of education, he was the first President of the Italian School Committee; in social action, he was fully engaged in the establishment of FACI. On several occasions, he did not hesitate to stand openly and effectively alongside those who were committed to the acquisition of rights and opportunities for all.

Fr. Nicola De Angelis, from the region of Latina, began his pastoral work humbly as assistant pastor and then pastor of St. Sebastian's Church in downtown Toronto. He was elected as a Trustee of the Catholic school board, and later was appointed director of development for the Archdiocese of Toronto. Fr. De Angelis, who was very active in the field of education, was among the pioneers of the teaching of the Italian language in Canada. His doctoral thesis in theology included a section on the pastoral importance of the mother tongue. He went to Italy for a few years before returning to Toronto as Auxiliary Bishop of the Archdiocese. Bishop De Angelis had an extraordinary capacity for communication within religious institutions as well as secular ones. It was a great surprise when, less than two years later, he was transferred from Toronto to Peterborough as bishop of that eastern Ontario town, where the Italian presence was almost non-existent. It was a strange transfer, indeed. Be that as it may, Monsignor De Angelis was a well-loved, and well respected person and one of great outreach to the community.

Another priest who was greatly involved in the social life of the community was Fr. Gianni Carparelli. He was the founder and the soul of Caritas in Toronto where for about 30 years he dedicated his life to its rehabilitation centre for young drug addicts. This was indeed an unconventional priest in every sense of the word. His action found a lot of success and widespread support in the community, but this did not help to make him more acceptable in the eyes of the chancery. He dreamed of a church nearer to the people. In the fall of 2012, somewhat discouraged, he decided to return to Italy.

One priest who no doubt left his mark was Fr. Benito Framarin. Possessing a somewhat higher cultural background than many immigrants, he openly criticized his colleagues, and would not tolerate mediocrity or the superficial. Notwithstanding his intellectual approach, he used simple and accessible language, while communicating a depth of content and analysis. He spent his time in Toronto alternating between pastoral ministry at Holy Angels Church in Etobicoke, and work as a professional journalist. He served as editorial director of the *Corriere Canadese* and *Il Samaritano*. Fr. Framarin valued dialogue, and was willing to exchange views with other religious and lay people, without hypocrisy or prejudice. His book, *I cattivi pensieri di Don Smarto – un prete italiano in Canada* (Edizioni Paduai: 1986) offers an interesting picture of the Toronto Italia of the 1960s and '70s. Although at times his reflections or syntheses are not widely shared, his analysis is always lucid and intelligent.

Fr. Giuseppe Carraro was one of the priests most engaged in issues of social justice, making him at times unpopular with his colleagues. In the 1950s, with Carletto Caccia, he was one of the founders of COSTI. This centre still plays a positive role for the immigrant community by offering English language classes, and helping skilled workers adapt to Canadian standards in their trades. At the same time as COSTI was started, another organization with strong ties to the Catholic Church played a significant part in assisting the newly-arrived. The Italian Immigrant Aid Society, headed by Isa Scotti, was also involved in social services. With the changing requirements of Italian immigration, however, this organization's existence was short-lived.

By the early seventies, a new consciousness took root among Italian priests who for decades had performed secondary roles within the parishes. Their impatience with the church hierarchy, the majority of whom were Irish, became more and more obvious. It should be noted that this malcontent among the Italian clergy began to occur at the same time in which FACI and the Congress were created and union activities intensified. Some results were not long in coming: many priests were finally appointed as pastors, and the Curia appointed its first vicar for the Italians in the person of Monsignor John Iverinci, a dynamic cleric who succeeded in a short time to attract attention in Catholic circles.

At that time, the Church held a very conservative stance, leaving little room for the more liberal wing. The most authoritative voice was that of Cardinal Aloysius Ambrozic, Archbishop of the Archdiocese of Toronto. The Italian Canadian clergy, for the most part, identified with his rather conservative agenda. A priest of the Old Guard who was capable of gaining the respect of many for his humanitarian approach and coherence with his principles, was Msgr. Giuseppe Sbrocchi. In those years a heated debate was unleashed around the refusal of administering the sacraments of First Communion and Confirmation to students who did not attend Catholic schools. It was certainly an unexpected estrangement for thousands of immigrant families from Italy who had not considered the choice of school for their children on religious grounds but based on convenience. They chose the schools close in proximity to their homes. The refusal of sacraments was denounced in both English and Italian media, resulting in protest and indignation. The debate lasted for a few years and ended with minimal results. What did allow the Catholic schools to prevail in the final choice was the new strategy of the Catholic school boards to include the teaching of the Italian language during regular school hours. This matter is dealt with extensively in the chapter devoted to Centro Scuola.

Generally speaking, religious affiliation in the Italian Canadian community is experienced more as a social practice than as a spiritual disposition. For the most part, church attendance is for the sake of family celebrations, weddings, funerals, etc., and for special ceremonies such as the liturgies of Easter and Christmas. In fact, priests still refer to these kinds of parishioners as the "pasqualini" (Easter-goers) and "natalini," (Christmas-goers). Many parish communities tend to maintain those traditions that bring everyone together, such as the festivities of patron saints, being unable to eliminate those folkloristic and banal practices that have little to do with the authentic expression of a true faith. Much different is the grand procession of Good Friday, which for decades has drawn to College Street, in the heart of Toronto, tens of thousands of spectators amazed and excited by the pathos expressed by the very stylized spectacle of a ritual as immutable as it is intensely felt by its protagonists

For the community today, there is a desire for some fresh air, to overcome any lack of communication between the Church and society, and for a more ecumenical and respectful dialogue in the ecclesial community. There is a wealth of history and traditions in the churches of Toronto, and in the fabric of the community. Gone is the need for separate sports leagues, for example, once seen as necessary to provide activities for children who had been on the margins. My hope is that the leadership of the new pontiff, Pope Francis, will be the model for church leaders around the globe. It seems appropriate to include His Holiness in this chapter because, after all, he is the son of Italian immigrants to Argentina. In particular, there is a phrase he addressed to the clergy which certainly applies to the priests in our community, and that is, "Teach the Gospel not with the rod but with love." There is a real need to adopt this beautiful phase from Papa Bergoglio.

TWELVE

Centro Scuola: Canadian Centre for Italian Culture and Education

IN THE WELL-KNOWN WORK, *Beyond the Melting Pot*, a picture was drawn that successfully summarizes a main driving force of the Centro Scuola e Cultura Italiana. Referring to the immigration situation in New York in the past, the authors Daniel P. Moynihan and Nathan Glazer noted that, while Italians celebrate Columbus, Garibaldi, etc., and build memorials, the Jewish communities build and manage schools, and hospitals. This observation could very well apply to the Canadian situation in the sixties. There's nothing wrong with celebrating Columbus and Garibaldi, of course. The mistake lies in believing that this is the attitude of most immigrants towards their Italian ancestry. It seemed to me important that the Italian essence be affirmed not out of nostalgia, but rather by the establishment in Canadian society of socially useful initiatives, which relate to the values of the cultural heritage of the motherland and at the same time look towards the future.

The Centro Scuola e Cultura Italiana was launched in Toronto in 1976. Those times were particular ones in Canadian history. There was a new cultural ferment then, giving rise to a truly Canadian vision that could be projected into the future. Thus began the commitment to create a genuinely Canadian identity. The many ethnic communities that make up Canadian society were influenced by this innovative way of thinking. They, too, began to regain their original identities. Problems posed by the dual identity and dual nationality gave rise to new research on how to overcome these. It was the Italians who pushed beyond what were economic difficulties and problems of social inclusion. We attempted to identify what were the most important needs, and we promoted initiatives that have had great significance and lasting impact on the history of immigration in Canada.

Some of the projects that came to life in those years were described in chapter 7: Villa Colombo, a magnificent residence for the elderly, and the Columbus Centre. However, these great accomplishments were not enough for us. It was important to preserve our cultural identity within the Canadian mosaic. To do this, we realized that language would have to play a fundamental role. Adopting the slogan, "a culture without a language is a culture without life," we began directing our efforts towards maintaining the Italian language, trying to insert it into the normal school day curriculum. Many groups in the past had tried to organize Italian classes. They did so in "pioneer" sort of ways; in the basements of churches, without any pedagogical coordination, without teaching aids, without a pedagogical strategy. Everything, though undoubtedly meritorious, appeared improvised.

We aimed instead to gain recognition for the teaching of languages, in our case Italian, as a fundamental component for the cognitive development of the child. We asked that Italian, and likewise other languages, be taught during regular school hours; that it be part of didactic activity in the school; that it be fully integrated into the school curriculum. It was very difficult to convince the school boards of this new vision of education, in the beginning. The community leaders understood that it was time to take the reins of our own destiny. We had to rely on our own strength and our own self-awareness. It was thanks to this realization and the strength of our own convictions that it was possible to develop any serious proposals. On this basis, a dialogue was initiated with school board authorities. Our position was clear and well-supported by several documents and pedagogical research. The knowledge of several languages is beneficial not only to the developing child, but it is of value to our national identity. Canada benefits from linguistic facility in diplomatic relations and economic networks. Further, it broadens our cultural horizons, and contributes to better understanding within our diverse Canadian population.

All of these arguments were contained in a brief to the Ontario Minister of Education, the Hon. Tom Wells, prepared by Centro Scuola and presented by the National Congress of Italian Canadians early in 1977. In May of that year, Premier William Davis and Minister Wells announced the creation of the Heritage Languages Program, including the budget to support the language classes. Although there was no provision to make it part of the regular school curriculum, the announcement was well received by different communities across Ontario. The legislation stipulated that requests for such programs would have to come from the parents.

Our position had prevailed, albeit not completely because while the classes could be offered during the regular school hours, they were not part of the school curriculum. The objective was getting closer to realization. First, it was necessary to gain the interest of the greatest number of parents and then to bring our activities to the schools where many claims of interest had been filed. We had to talk to parents and organize neighbourhood committees. In this way, it would be the parents that would be asking the schools to teach Italian. We could be the driving force, the organizers, but the request had to come from the parents. For the school boards, in short, it was important to accept a request, not to impose its will. We overcame many difficulties throughout the years, but the challenges continued to sprout like mushrooms. Every time a financial crisis appeared on the horizon, the first program that the school boards wanted to cut was the teaching of heritage languages. Of course, we were always able to defend ourselves by virtue of the principle that we were paying taxes in Canada and that Canada had an obligation towards us. We also succeeded in convincing the Italian government to accept this transparent arrangement where we asked them for financial aid to manage independently in conjunction with the Canadian funding; that is, we asked for help so that we might all invest in the future of the Italian-Canadian community, refusing however, to be handled and directed.

As the programs developed, we organized professional development days for our instructors, under the title "Heritage Languages Symposium." Over the years this conference grew, taking in participants from all the school boards in the Greater Toronto Area. For 15 years we were able to organize workshops on teaching methodology for as many as 1,000 teachers of 42 different languages. Likewise, we created new initiatives for students, adding secondary school classes to the existing courses at the primary and intermediate levels. The instructors collaborate with universities through research activities. I consider of paramount importance what we have done and continue to do to develop new teaching strategies for young people of the third and fourth generation.

To support the courses and teacher development, we undertook a commitment to produce teaching materials. The books that came from Italy did not reflect the progression of language and grammar of children of second and third generation. In addition, the images and concepts of those books did not reflect Canadian values and the environment, generating serious learning difficulties. Instead, the manuals produced by us were highly successful. This does not mean that we reject what comes from Italy. Quite the contrary; we welcome the great amount of excellent teaching aids that come to us from Italy. Our manuals are well matched to Italian ones, especially since more innovative texts, closer to the reality of today, are available. The results have always proven us right and they are our best calling card. Currently, some 30,000 students in Toronto take courses of Italian language and culture. In addition, we have reached a formal agreement with the local school boards so that the courses are managed in partnership by pooling our resources with those from the school boards and with some financial contributions from the Italian government.

We realized at a certain point that classroom teaching was no longer enough; the first thing that came to mind was creating programs based on visits to Italy. In particular, we conceived the idea of having courses in Italian culture abroad, supported by Canadian school boards. We started by organizing language study abroad in Italy for short periods of time. The results were excellent and they continue to be significant. The charm of Italy, as well as facilitating the refinement of language skills, is generally able to generate huge cultural stimulation. Subsequently, we proposed to the school boards that residential courses held in Italy be recognized as credit courses towards the secondary school diplomas. In this too we found immediate success. At present, participating schools are implementing curricular courses in Italy with Canadian teachers, paid by their school boards, for Canadian students, and not necessarily of Italian ancestry. The courses are of one month in the summer or four months in the fall. To date nearly 10,000 young people have taken part in this program, and so have become familiar with Italian culture and its rich civilization.

An issue that seems to me of great significance concerns the children of the younger generation, those who know just as much of Italy their parents or grandparents tell them. They live a reality which is basically Canadian. The Canadian reality is something in itself and Canadians care about standing apart from the Americans and the British. Currently, the young Italian Canadian is well aware of his or her identity. However, national identity is not everything. Cultural identity is just as important. What I've always held as an indispensable goal is to make it possible for Italian Canadian youth to be proud of their cultural roots, and that they come to know their historical and human background. It is to this end that Centro Scuola works to raise awareness of both their language and the cultural heritage of Italy. The language courses bring about a profound transformation in young people. They sometimes arrive in Italy without much enthusiasm and then they are astonished and become impassioned when their eyes and their minds discover the Italy of today: their Italian peers, the great civilization of the past, the history, the art, the Ferrari, the fashion, and so on. When they return to Canada they seem truly proud, and they begin to want to speak the language that before perhaps they ignored or even scorned. Speaking Italian becomes the reason for social excellence and pride.

Centro Scuola has also played a major role in the field of cultural promotion, accomplished by enabling a significant publishing activity, giving rise to two polyphonic choirs, and offering courses in dance, music and song. The Palestrina Chamber Chorus was founded in September, 1997 and soon became one of the best Canadian choirs composed of young people between 18 and 30 years of age. The choir toured Italy several times, performed together with the Toronto Symphony Orchestra, and sang for Pope John Paul II during his visit to Canada. The choir also recorded two CDs. Another choir of children's voices, the Schola Cantorum, performed side by side with the Palestrina. This children's choir was designed to encourage even the youngest to learn the language and culture, since the ultimate aim of all the activities of the Centro Scuola remains that of promoting language and culture. For a decade the two choirs combined to present thrilling concerts at Christmas time and again in the spring. The repertoire included choral works by Palestrina, Pergolesi, Vivaldi, Bach and Mozart, as well as charming contemporary songs in English and in Italian. The Centro Scuola singers had the opportunity to train with excellent music teachers such as Ermanno Mauro, one of the legendary tenors of the Metropolitan Opera of New York. This created a lively and stimulating environment, enabling students to achieve consistently good results. The dance classes were also popular and successful, including ballet, jazz, and musical theatre. The teaching was entrusted to professionals of international stature, having trained in Europe and North America.

Our pledge to publish material dedicated to the Italian-Canadian culture has been one of the most appreciated contributions of Centro Scuola to the cultural life of Canada. Starting from 1979, many volumes of literary interest have been published, such as: *The Culture of Italy, Medieval to Modern*, a collection of essays edited by Bernard Chandler and Julius A. Molinaro; *Italian Canadian Voices: An Anthology of Poetry and Prose*, edited by Caroline Morgan Di Giovanni, in two editions, 1984 and 2006; *Love's Sinning Song and Other Poems*, a collection of poems of the Toronto poet, Celestino De Iuliis. Centro Scuola has also published important work on the history of immigration; among others: *Dalla frontiera alle Little Italies 1800–1945*, by Robert F. Harney; *The Luminous Mosaic: Italian Cultural Organizations in Ontario*, edited by Julius A. Molinaro and Maddalena Kuitunen; *From the Shores of Hardship: Italians in Canada*, a posthumous work of Robert F. Harney, edited by Nicholas De Maria Harney. In 1984, Centro Scuola founded the academic journal, *Italian Canadiana*, edited by Julius A. Molinaro. In 1988, the journal was integrated into the Department of Italian Studies, University of Toronto, then, in 1995, it became part of the Frank Iacobucci Centre for Italian Canadian Studies, at U. of T.

The headquarters of the Centro Scuola at the Columbus Centre has been enriched by a library that bears my name, a library of which I was the founder and the largest contributor. It holds thousands of volumes of material on Italian subjects, in English or in Italian, and consists of important specialized sections devoted to Italian history, art, and literature and Italian Canadian writers. Next to the library is a museum with fine artefacts from Italy, including numerous objects illustrating Italian civilization, some specimens in mosaic; beautiful ceramics from different regions; masks of the *commedia dell'arte*; a room dedicated to Leonardo da Vinci with life-size reproductions of paintings; facsimile parchment manuscripts; examples of Venetian glass; and other historic arts and crafts. Of special interest is the fascinating collection of nativity scenes from all over the world.

The mandate of Centro Scuola speaks of the promotion of Italian culture in Canada. To this end, I undertook sponsorships of some important art exhibitions and performances in the cultural milieu of metropolitan Toronto. At the Carrier Gallery in the Columbus Centre, we helped to bring a display of the works of Raffaello from the Vatican, in June, 1984. Again at the Carrier Gallery, we mounted the Leonardo: Arte, Scienza, e Utopia exhibit in May, 1987. Centro Scuola sponsored a performance of Rossini's *La Cenerentola* with the Canadian Opera Company under Richard Bradshaw, in April, 1996. The Centro logo also appeared as the sponsor for a production of Prokofief's *Romeo and*

Juliet, by the National Ballet in February, 1998. Then, in an initiative to link the great legacy of Dante Alighieri with contemporary per-formers, Centro Scuola presented staged presentations by actors and musicians. The first, in October, 2005, showcased the Italian stars Ugo Pagliai and Paola Gassman, with Canadian Jennifer Dale and the string quartet Solisti di Toronto. Upon the opening of the Casa Dante exhibit of rare editions and paintings based on the *Divine Comedy, (La Divina Commedia)*, in May, 2006, we presented another program combining spoken recitations by Antonia Serrao-Soppelsa, and music by pianist Nazzareno Caruso, who gave an extraordinary performance of the Dante Cantata by Franz Liszt. A third production combining Dante's poetry with music featured Ugo Pagliai and Paolo Gassman, once again, with Canadian actor Tony Nardi, and the Italian Baroque musicians of the Ensemble Benedetto Marcello. The standard of excellence for all of these events helped to create enthusiastic audiences year after year.

In 2009, a new relationship developed between Centro Scuola and the Tafelmusik Baroque Orchestra. The generous musicians of this fine, world class period instrument ensemble rushed forward to offer a free concert to support fundraising efforts after the devastating earth-quake in l'Aquila. The concert took place on June 2, 2009, the Italian National Day, in the Walker Court of the Art Gallery of Ontario. It thrilled the capacity audience, and helped to raise $10,000 for the cause. After this, Centro Scuola sponsored a performance of the spec-tacular *Galileo Project,* a combination of music from the time of the great Italian astronomer, with projections of deep space captured by the Hubble telescope. This amazing orchestra continues to perform reper-toire that includes many Italian composers of the Baroque period, such as Vivaldi, Monteverdi, Sanmartini, Boccherini, Albinoni, and many others. The Toronto Italian community should patronize this particular ensemble which is dedicated to keeping this grand musical tradition fresh and alive for every generation.

With its quest for developing new strategies for motivating students of the second and third generation, we developed a new symbiosis between language classes and sport activities. It began in 1982, the year of the triumphant victory of Italy at the World Cup. The enthusiasm which erupted across Toronto on that occasion was truly memorable. On the evening of the victory a large crowd, the largest ever seen in Toronto, gathered on Saint Clair Avenue West, between Bathurst St. and Lansdowne Avenue. This long and wide street, at one time raucous and somewhat shoddy but now elegant and sparkling, has long been one of the main points of reference for the Italian-Canadian community. There were thousands of Italians celebrating the soccer victory, of course, but it seemed like a dream to see the huge number of Anglophones, Francophones, Chinese, South Americans, blacks and races of every kind, and Europeans of the most diverse affiliations. At that point, as the passion for soccer spread, we were deluged by so many requests from kids and parents that we could not help but come up with something that might provide the answer to that wave of enthusiasm.

Our musings led us to conclude that the encouragement of serious study of the mother tongue of parents and grandparents was not enough. We needed to engage our young people, and hold their interest. To succeed, it was necessary to combine learning the language with Italian culture. So, we started with soccer lessons to teach the fundamentals of the sport, and then we formed many teams, divided groups by age, and started the practice of having tournaments. These first began as Centro Scuola in house matches, advanced to the various district competitions and then ended with arriving at official championships.

Further development came by including other sports rather than just soccer, and from this sprang the idea, at first rather far-fetched, of bringing our athletes to participate in the Giochi della Gioventú, or Youth Games, held every year in Italy by CONI, the Italian National Olympic Committee. Thanks to the dedication of two outstanding educators, we participated, taking home a number of medals every time. Vittorio Angelosante, a physical education teacher and school principal with the MSSB (the Toronto Catholic District School Board) first convinced the school boards to lend their support, then he organized and trained the original teams of intermediate-level students. After his tragic early death, his colleague Phil Riddell, also a Catholic school principal, took over the annual project, training and preparing students under 14 years old for the trip overseas and the international competition. The first gold medal came in 1986, with our own soccer team coached by Santino Di Giovanni. Our euphoric excitement was no less disbelieving than that of the Italian coaches, technicians and journalists who recorded the triumph on home ground of the boys who came from a country which was never listed as one of soccer greats. During the winter months, we created other opportunities for socialization and cultural growth.

Throughout the year, there were student trips to Italy, not only to compete in sport competitions, but most of all to be exposed to the rich tradition of art and history. This was true educational travel: the practice of sport and the study of language; cheering for our team colours and visiting museums and concert halls; getting an earthy whiff of soccer fields and then savouring the beauty of monuments and landscapes from one end of Italy to another. I remember the stunned faces and the smug comments of quite a few people, that time in Padua when our kids in their sport uniforms came out from a visit to the Scrovegni Chapel happy and well-behaved. People were struck by seeing so many young athletes impressed by the masterly frescoes of Giotto. The Centro Scuola teams were so energized by this successful combination that we continued to enter tournaments and friendly competitions with young teams in almost every region of "the Boot," making new discoveries and creating indelible memories.

This unique reality of Canada did not go unnoticed in Italy. In 1994, CONI responded to Canadian requests with a number of financial interventions aimed at encouraging the promotion of sports among young Italians abroad. For the first time, CONI itself assumed responsibility in covering the cost of air travel for young people from countries overseas. The new funding allowed the Coordination Committee of CONI Canada to expand their activities and to arrive at actively involving up to 10,000 young people every year. In 1995 we reached the pinnacle of sporting success with the "Centro Scuola Sport" graduating as Italian champions and winners of the Youth Games overall. We even had the satisfaction of ending up on the front pages of major Italian sports dailies. In total, the young Italian Canadians won as many as 15 Medals: 7 Gold, 6 Silver and 2 Bronze. That affirmation resounded long, and in June 1997 the President of CONI, Mario Pescante, visited Toronto to observe first-hand what it was that we were doing. At the same time, we received the visit of the then President of the Republic, Oscar Luigi Scalfaro. That season of the Youth Games for Canada remains an unforgettable moment in history. In 1999, the Youth Games entered the beginning of a new phase, which saw the general organization entrusted to the Italian Ministry of Education. *I Giochi della Gioventú* (The youth games) in its new format took on the name of *Giochi Sportivi Studenteschi* (the Student Sports Games).

Centro Scuola also won many laurels in Canada, repeatedly becoming champions of Ontario and once even champions of Canada. As Carmine Isacco, Sporting Director of the University of Toronto and Centro Scuola once stated:

> *It is fair to say, however, that the best victory is never represented by the trophy, the medals and the hosannas sung by the public and the press, but rather by looks of those kids who, victorious or not, when they come back from Italy have a new awareness of their roots and the desire to return as soon as possible, to be immersed in the language and the traditions from which they would have been hopelessly cut off without the magnificent combination of sport and culture made possible by Centro Scuola.*

Now, Italy is more widely appreciated as a result of what Canadian students report in their daily conversations within their family, at school and elsewhere. They talk about how they were greeted with warmth and kindness, the friendships born with their Italian peers, the beauty of the cities and the charm of its natural habitats, of having experienced the sensation of feeling at home, and the regret with which they faced the moment of parting at the end of their stay in Italy. It is with the greatest pleasure, for us who live in Canada, to see how many young people are attracted by the opportunity to discover the land and the culture of origin of their parents and grandparents. In some ways it is no less exciting to see how the attraction for Italy is also born and develops in youngsters who have little or nothing to do with an Italian origin, and who in increasing numbers, turn out to be among the participants of activities of Centro Scuola carried out in Canada, as well as those that take place in Italy.

Centro Scuola has been and remains at the heart of the Italian-Canadian community of Toronto, both because it is home to so much testimony of the life, culture and traditions of Italy, and for the impetus that it provides to the cultural scene. One of the major reasons for our success has been the undertaking of Centro Scuola's journey towards this great adventure with a group of volunteer advisors who, not coincidentally, have played distinctive roles in Canadian society. I want to mention in particular, among others, the Irish Dominican Father Leonard Boyle, who taught at the Pontifical Institute of Medieval Studies in Toronto and then became Prefect of the Vatican Library; Tony Silipo who was a Member of the Provincial Parliament of Ontario and Minister of Education in the government of Bob Rae; Rev. Nicola De Angelis, a parish priest in Toronto, who was elected a trustee on the Metropolitan Separate School Board of Toronto (later the Toronto Catholic District School Board) and who had included in his doctoral thesis in theology a section on the importance of heritage languages for school age children, and was named Bishop of Peterborough. Right from the beginning, we had within our fold, some leading academics, such as linguist Gianrenzo Clivio; scholar Julius Molinaro, and the already recognized historian, Robert Harney. The following extraordinary personalities cannot be forgotten: Dr. Renzo Carbone, one of the few professionals both socially and culturally involved in the community; Fabio Rizi, of whom we have already spoken; the lawyer, Frank Soppelsa , a former professor of Italian at the University of Toronto and former professional soccer player; the pharmacist, Dr. Laureano Leone, then member of Ontario's Parliament and Chairman of the National Congress of Italian Canadians; Sam Marafioti, another noteworthy trustee on the Catholic

School Board in Toronto; the writer Celestino De Iuliis; Anna Marie Castrilli, a lawyer and also a member of the Ontario Legislature.

Today one can certainly recognize how the good work of the past has also yielded the seeds for the future.

THIRTEEN

The Furore over "Ethnic" Languages

THE PROBLEM OF LANGUAGES EDUCATION has always been a source of controversy and a major obstacle in the formation of the national identity. It is difficult to understand the importance of the language issue, if no account is taken of the events that agitated the history of modern Canada, in particular the tension between the newly-formed Provinces and the central government created in 1867. It may suffice, as an example, to dwell on the first major crisis which erupted after Confederation on the issue of languages education. The crisis flared in the province of Manitoba, created in 1870 with a population divided equally between Francophones and Anglophones.

The seven Mennonite Elders who visited Manitoba in 1873 received a memorandum from Mr. Lowe, the Secretary of the Federal Department of Agriculture, setting among the conditions of immigration a clause which allowed them the privilege of educating their children in their native German language. On the strength of this, there was an influx of Mennonite settlers coming into Manitoba through the late 1870s. As the province expanded, other groups joined the population. In 1890, the language of instruction privileges were repealed, not only for the Mennonites but for the French-speaking Manitobans as well. The Manitoba Schools Act established that except for English, the teaching of languages did not fall within the duty of the public purse. This provision included the suppression of financing for public schools which were Catholic and Francophone, arising from the fear of Anglophone Manitoba seeing its cultural and political hegemony erode.

One must keep in mind the undeniably close bond that existed between linguistic expression and religious belief at the end of the 1800s. There was a complicated sequence of conflicting stances, public demonstrations, riots and political negotiations. The case in Manitoba did not remain a local issue: it quickly inflamed public opinion of the whole of Canada, enough to become the key element in the federal elections of 1896. The Conservative Party, in power for decades, was defeated. Thanks to the diplomacy of the newly-elected Prime Minister Wilfred Laurier, on November 16, 1896, a compromise was reached with Premier Greenway, described in Article 2, section 10, of the Manitoba Schools Act. The wording is as follows:

(10) Where ten of the pupils in any school speak the French language (or any language other than English) as their native language, the teaching of such pupils shall be conducted in French (or such other language), and English upon the bilingual system.

This historic accord could have been the model for Canada's future. It was so successful that, in 1910, over 40% of Manitoba's schoolchildren were enrolled in bilingual schools. But the results of the policy did not achieve the hoped-for consensus among the general population, despite the fact that even Pope Leo XIII himself had recognized that the compromise between Laurier and the Premier of Manitoba constituted the only reasonable chance of satisfactory settlement of the dispute.

Then, throughout the years of the Great War, the situation began to deteriorate progressively along with a mounting wave of hysteria against the teaching of the languages spoken by peoples considered "enemies." The final blow came in 1920 with the ultimate elimination of all forms of bilingual education, and the proclamation of English as the only official language, apart from the case of the inextinguishable

French in Quebec. It wasn't until the 1970s that the reintroduction in Canada of the teaching of languages other than English would take place. This would not be a simple and painless process.

There was another issue that had to be considered before the events that led to the introduction of the teaching of Italian in Ontario public schools at the elementary level. This was the campaign to end a serious discriminatory practice in secondary schools. Specifically, it concerned the disproportionate number of Italian and immigrant students who were channelled into the vocational schools. Until the early seventies, Italian students were steered in large numbers towards vocational schools, those schools that offered skills training, preparing the students to enter the labour market without further education. All that was required was to learn a trade, any trade, that could place them directly into the workforce.

It was not mandatory, of course, that one end up in the cultural meat grinder of vocational schools, but circumstances made it so. In the first place, assuming that the parents had little or no knowledge of English, bad counsel was deliberately given at the stage when the choice of school was to be made for the student. Even more perverse, some methods resulted in humiliating the students. For example, aptitude tests were to determine selection. The type of test which was to remain typical of this time was "the toaster" test. The student was shown a picture of a toaster and was asked to say what it was, and what that object was used for. These young people who had never in their lives seen or tasted sliced white bread, much less seen a toaster, of course remained silent. This then served to demonstrate that ignorance of an object as simple and of such common use in any Canadian home precluded any aptitude for a future different from that obtainable through training in vocational schools. We were able to put an end to that system in the interest of the growth not only of Italian newcomers but also of the children of immigrants from all other backgrounds. Today, there are many ways to give opportunities for a productive future to any student, of any ethnicity, who may not wish to pursue an academic course of study.

One of the actions taken to expose this malpractice of sending the children of immigrants into schools without opportunities for growth was the presentation of the document "The immigrant child and the Vocational Schools" at the Toronto Board of Education on March 5, 1973. The document was the result of careful study and elaboration and was promoted by FACI, the Canadian Federation of Italian Associations and Clubs. It contained, among other things, a statement of fundamental importance:

> *Education for every child is a fact of Canadian life. Most of the immigrants who arrive in Canada have come specifically to provide a better standard of living for their offspring. In this society education is often the key to social success; therefore, to have a child denied the chance for a better education simply because his parents did not understand the alternatives is injustice of the higher order.*

Similarly to what we did in the case of vocational schools, the battle for the teaching of Italian in Canadian schools was not only about what happened in our own backyard. From the beginning, we have always been concerned with and fought for the inclusion of all modern languages within the regular school curriculum. This was one of the most inspired insights of our movement, having shaped a formidable alliance of considerable strength. To understand the challenge, one must grasp what difficulties were encountered in the struggle for the teaching of languages in Ontario public schools. The most intense and fierce phase began in 1977. Until that time, all that we had been able to obtain were a few periods of teaching each week, in afternoon or weekend time slots, with optional participation. Instead, we now aimed to achieve the inclusion of modern languages in curricular programs.

It was necessary to clarify for the general public that the desire for Italian classes came from Italian Canadians who were local taxpayers, and whose children were born in Canada, in the majority. Their aim and objective was to enrich themselves culturally, broaden their horizons and strengthen their family connections. The children of immigrants should be able to converse with the older generation. The accusations about language education being rooted in nationalistic emotions, and dividing communities into ghettos, was simply hogwash. We could hardly understand how such fears came about. Besides, facility in other languages is a positive factor in extending economic opportunities for international trade. My commitment to this issue led to my election as spokesperson for the Metro Communities for International Languages.

The debate lasted a long time between hits, misses, and new accomplishments, until the final stabilizing of its results, gained almost in sight of the new millennium. There was considerable media attention at all stages of the debate. I am not referring only to the ethnic newspapers, radio, TV and print, but by the English-language media as well. The attention given by the *Toronto Star*, the newspaper that since 1892 is one of the most authoritative voices of journalism in Canada, was particularly substantial in following this issue. On October 20, 1976, the *Toronto Star* clearly summed up some aspects of the new educational directions resulting from the introduction of the Heritage Language Program by the Metro Toronto Separate School Board (now called the Toronto Catholic District School Board):

> *The Board's new policy emphasizes making staff aware of the needs and aspirations of ethnic communities, improving relations with them through a network of school-community workers and teaching languages other than English and French at the secondary level. At the elementary level, the Board supports using other languages in transition courses until a child learns English, and bringing discussion of ethnic groups into traditional subjects.*

In reporting that many leaders and teachers of the school system *"feel ethnic studies overburden the teachers, hamper English instruction and create ghettos in the school,"* the newspaper offered considerable prominence to our points of view:

Toronto teachers and principals who are opposed to helping children from immigrant families maintain their language and culture are out of touch with reality, according to ethnic community leaders.

In particular, The Star reported statements made by members of the Greek and Polish communities and earlier observations that I had been asked to make in the capacity as President of the Dante Society of Toronto:

Teachers who oppose ethnic studies today are overreacting to a situation they fail to understand. The Board of Education is on the right track because they've finally understood the new educational needs in our society. They shouldn't look at ethnic studies on a nationality basis. The immigrants understand they're Canadians now. But teachers must recognize the cultural pluralism in our world.

As it should be, a voice was also given to those who thought differently, such as the president of the Parent-Teacher Council of Eastdale Secondary School, who claimed: "*I'm not being bigoted, but I feel we have to draw the line somewhere,*" since "*we have reports of university students who can't write an English essay. If they're having trouble with English, why have them study another language?*" From statements made by the Trustees of the Toronto School Board, however, there emerged both lucidity and wisdom. Dan Leckie had this to say: "*Obviously, any change is threatening for a little while.*" Irene Atkinson declared: "*People don't generally realize how alienated these children are when they arrive here. We have to provide some sort of bridge between the home and school.*" My experience as a community educator allowed me to understand both the problems of a didactic nature and the needs of families and students.

That was a time of great anguish. It was incumbent upon us to make clear that we knew English and that our children knew English as well, if not better, than many young people from English-speaking families. We had to make it clear that the matter was an entirely different one: that our aim was to keep alive our cultural heritage; that that legacy would be an enrichment useful not only to our children but to the entire Canadian society. These are very easy concepts to understand nowadays. But, in the seventies, these same concepts were difficult to grasp. However, with both perseverance and good comportment we were able to go forward and find success.

In February of 1977, we submitted a memorandum to the Minister of Education of Ontario, Tom Wells, in which, among other things, we advised that *"The Government of Ontario should make a clear statement of interest, concern and support for educational and cultural projects proposed by appropriate organizations in the Italian sector, to be expressed in relevant legislation."* The following May 4, Premier William Davis announced the start of a new policy and the allocation of substantial funds for the teaching of the "third language." However, the essence of that announcement left us perplexed and disappointed, so much so that I and other members of the Committee for the Accreditation of Third Languages in Ontario laid out a series of observations, which in summary went like this:

> *Frankly, in its present form, the Heritage Language Program simply does not meet the legitimate cultural-linguistic rights of a significant number of the population of Ontario. Unless serious amendments are made to the newly announced Program, we sincerely feel that the creditability of Ontario's commitment to multiculturalism will be seriously undermined.*

Along with me, as representative of the National Congress of Italian-Canadians, Athanassios Foussias also signed for the Greek community, Imants Purvs for Latvians, Michael Wawryshyn for Ukrainians, and Ruth Lee for the Spanish-speaking community.

The ambiguity of the Ontario government favoured the revival of public opinion that was against multiculturalism. At the start of the new school year, some Anglophone parents threatened to go on strike. The *Toronto Star*, on November 1, 1977, reported that "*angry parents across Metro will keep their children home from school for a day*" if "*the policy on foreign language classes during the day is not changed.*" The main argument in support of the protesters was that the part of the normal school hours allocated to the teaching of a third language would have taken away valuable learning time, to which they had a right, from the students.

On 22 November, the *Toronto Star* took a firm position that cut the Gordian knot. In one of the reports dedicated to the issue, I was cited, this time in my capacity as director of the Centro Scuola e Cultura Italiana:

> Parents are complaining about Heritage Language courses
> through prejudice or bigotry. Most of the things they are saying
> simply aren't true. We would never be in favour of the language
> programs if they would endanger the learning of English. We
> want to be integrated. We want to make it in Canada. Studies
> have shown the foreign language reinforces a student's learning
> skills for other subjects. It creates a better psychological envi-
> ronment for the child when there is no conflict at home – because
> of communication difficulties – or within the child. He does not
> have to ask "Who am I?"

The final blow to the protest movement came on that same day with the editorial. With the heading *Helping immigrant youth adjust*, the article presented unequivocal arguments, starting with, assuming that the protesters would eventually succeed, it "*would be a severe blow to multi-cultural education in Toronto,*" and ending with the solemn confirmation:

> Long ago, Canada decided it would not be a 'melting pot' like the
> United States. We chose not to boil off a man's native ways and
> pressure him to be a cultural clone of his neighbour. Instead, we
> preferred to be a nation of two official languages and a mighty

mosaic of cultures and religions. We are the happier and the richer for it.

New alarming crises followed in the early eighties because of the threat of budget cuts that would have led to the cancellation of the teaching of the "third language." A teachers' strike also demanded the elimination of the "third language" from the regular school timetable. The issue went well beyond the officially alleged wage claims: it was, in this case, a real ideological boycott against the Heritage Language Program. With strong determination, we challenged that attempt to rid politics of multiculturalism, and found true allies within the other communities, from Spanish and Portuguese to Greek and Chinese. A great demonstration sprang up outside the headquarters of the Toronto Board of Education, thanks to which all those who needed to understand knew perfectly well at that moment what was to be done to resolve the crisis.

Such blatant evidence offered the *Toronto Star* the opportunity to present an overview of the entire course of the multi-year affair. In the March 29, 1983 edition, the paper devoted a long article to my actions, headlined *"He carries the torch for heritage courses."* The writer, Hamlin Grange, wrote:

> *Language is an important part of any culture, says Alberto Di Giovanni, and for the past six years he has been fighting to have Italian taught to students as part of the regular curriculum in Metro schools. It hasn't been an easy task but Di Giovanni loves challenges. Making heritage languages – other than English and French – part of the regular school day has been a hot issue for the past six years and Di Giovanni has been at the centre ... Di Giovanni says the critics don't understand the aims of the program and many of them are 'bigots.' He says: 'North Americans have been accustomed to looking at the world one way, but now they will have to realize there are other people living among them. I don't deal with the bigots. You can't. You deal with people who*

aren't knowledgeable of the issue and sensitize them to create dialogue.'

Difficulties of every sort, and attempts to revoke "third language" teaching, came one after another almost every year. In early December of 1993 I prepared a study which the Centro Scuola e Cultura Italiana, in agreement with the Canadian Society for Italian Studies, the Dante Society of Toronto and the Canadian Italian Business and Professional Association, hoped to finally arrive at a pivotal moment through the Royal Commission on Learning of the government of Ontario. Some of the key topics in the document were the following:

We want our children to have a realistic and inclusive introduc-tion to history that identifies all the great civilizations of the world. Our children must understand their nation, Canada. They must have a knowledge and awareness of the history and civiliza-tion of the native people, the historic traditions of the French and English in Canada and the social and cultural contribution made by people who came from all over the globe. That is the approach to geography and history that our children need. They need to see themselves and all their neighbours having a vital role in the world of today ... The findings of a considerable number of recent studies suggest that additive forms of bi/trilingualism can posi-tively influence academic and cognitive functioning. There is also evidence that bi/trilingual children are better able to analyse lin-guistic communication than unilingual children. We suggest that availability of international languages in elementary schools, as part of the total educational process, will not only benefit the child now, but also in the future as Canada's international role expands and communication in different languages becomes a necessity.

The statistical data already in the early nineties showed the extraor-dinary results we were to achieve. Over 100,000 students from eighty backgrounds are registered annually in the schools of the Toronto

Catholic District School Board. Thirty-three percent of students attend language courses, of which 60% are for the study of Italian, looked after by from 50 to 60 teachers of mother tongue. The other four languages included in the regular curriculum are Portuguese, Polish, Spanish and Ukrainian, with percentages of participation at 11% and down. For a score of other languages, there are courses taught in the afternoon hours and on Saturday.

Learning Italian was not less important than learning English, because the shared mastery of the mother tongue is the necessary prerequisite to overcome the social fragmentation that results from the inability to communicate between countrymen. It prevents the formation of a collective consciousness capable of generating that identifying spirit which is essential in order not to succumb to a highly competitive and culturally foreign environment. The need for Italians transplanted abroad to learn their mother tongue has research documentation that dates back to 1841. It was then that Giuseppe Mazzini founded the Italian School of London, an initiative designed to give hundreds of young Italians the minimal communication tools needed to defend themselves from the abuse and violence of that environment by unscrupulous exploiters that we all know through Charles Dickens' Oliver Twist.

For adult Italians in Canada things were a little less difficult than in the London of Dickens and Mazzini: lend an ear here, a bit of sharp wit there, and somehow we all got through to communicating with each other, in Italian, English and even the various dialects. From this collective effort of oral interaction there slowly developed a phrasebook of survival which, once we grasped that the difficult to pronounce "pick and shovel" was the English for "picco e pala," we simplified and made ourselves understood by saying "pic-en-sciàbol." Similarly, from "park the car" and "parcheggia l'automobile" we arrived at "parca lu carru"; from "candy" and "caramella" was born "chenda"; and "the cake," aka "la torta," became "la checca." It was thus that the language of Italian Canadians, over the years, came to be a more adapted English, while the Italian (or what little of it existed at the time of landing in Canada) regressed to a battered and often comical jargon, always hovering between dialects, a blend of old-fashioned Italian and bastardized English.

For children, teens and young adults, things proceeded much differently: in school and university quality English was being learned, which yielded excellent skills in all curricular subjects, eliminating shyness, embarrassment and reluctance, and paving the way towards a lively social life and work advancement, free from any inferiority complex.

Do we all become Anglophones and send to the shredder all residue of that Italy from whose constraints we have had to flee? At first, yes. "Yes" was the answer that almost all the Italian immigrants understood and to which they conformed. In fact, why evade assimilation within the fabric of Anglophone society? Work, good or bad, was there; the general situation, by and large, was fine. We were good and valued citizens. Subsequently, the general sentiment changed direction: to be "Canadian" was no longer enough; still feeling affection and perfect loyalty to our new home, we wanted to be proud "Italian Canadians." What had happened?

Young people in school discovered the magnificence and grandeur of Italy, its ancient history, its heritage of beauty, ingenuity and creativity. Something similar happened to parents and grandparents, who, among co-workers, neighbours and friends, re-discovered feelings of veneration, if not envy, for their distant homeland, which they had for too long ignored, and for the splendid side of the stereotype they'd been forced to wear. And so, slowly, they began to backpedal. The new watchwords became: recover, rediscover, find again, do not lose, do not deny, do not forget! From that point on, the cultivation of the Italian language has become the preferred way not to abandon, but rather, to strengthen the bond with the land of their ancestors and with that civilization which in centuries past had been master of the world.

Would this turnaround have been possible and, above all, would it have had the success we all recognize today, if the link between the Italian language and the younger generation had been broken; if the battle for the teaching Italian in Canadian schools had not been invented, fought and won; if the Italian Canadians had not been able to oppose the fury against "ethnic" languages displayed by the most reactionary Anglophone circles, with their inflexible, calm and well-argued action for constructive dialogue?

I would like to end this chapter by acknowledging the great contributions given in those difficult days by prominent educators such as Steve Corvese, Superintendent of Continuing Education with the MSSB/Toronto Catholic District School Board; Tony Succi, principal with the same Board; Miriam De Giuseppe with the Toronto Board of Education; Giovanni Tullo, with the York Board of Education; Alba Bravoco, with the York Region Catholic District School Board; and the many dedicated instructors such as Tonia Ciprietti, Rosanna Senatore, Clara Ceolin, Domenico Servello, Luca Buiani, Angela Baldassarre-La Civita, Maria Di Ruscio, and many other loyal and dedicated teachers. They have my lasting gratitude for their outstanding service.

In conclusion, the struggle for an effective and fruitful language education is far from over. Language education can only provide full benefits if it is part of the regular curriculum, and particularly if it is offered under the terms of the bilingual model. Not only would students benefit from such enriched language facility, but the nation would gain from a population capable of doing business around the globe. Speaking several languages could become a proud Canadian distinction.

FOURTEEN

The Role of the Media

Mass media has always played an important role in Canadian society. With such a large land mass to cover, newspapers provided critical information to bring the regions together. Even Marconi's telegraph has a place in this story, with the first overseas signals sent from a hill near Halifax. Canada gave birth to Marshall McLuhan, the perceptive thinker who analysed the effects of communication on society and on the individual, and invented the popular dictum, "The medium is the message." With the wealth of media in everyday Canadian life, such a vast and important element as Italian culture could not be overlooked. After the wave of newcomers arrived in the post-war years, their stories began to appear in newspaper headlines, periodicals, and also on radio and television. At first the English language media ignored this population; however, the community was well served by journalists and entrepreneurs in the Italian language. In this rich and varied landscape two figures stand out as the pioneers in the emergence of media in the Italian-Canadian community: Dan Iannuzzi and Johnny Lombardi.

In 1954, Dan Iannuzzi founded the newspaper *Corriere Canadese* and then undertook the creation of the broadcasting stations MTV and Channel 47, the first network of multicultural Canada. The *Corriere Canadese*, however, remained the master opus of his life, an achievement that, after 35 years of constant and generous dedication, allowed him to transform the paper into a daily, anticipated by a wide readership. In the editorial of April 2, 1990, the first release of the new daily edition, he wrote that his was *"a newspaper that interprets reality, a journal just for information, opinions and intervention; a newspaper written in both Italian and in English."* The reason for this particularity, he explains in the English version of the editorial, was: *"To serve both first generation readers and their children, who are now poised to become leaders in business, the professions and their community."* He then added, that the new *Corriere Canadese* intended to be *"a newspaper for Canadians who take pride in their heritage."*

I like transcribing the passage of that editorial in which Iannuzzi mentions collaborators called to contribute to the "Editorials" page. I like it not only because it also bears my name, but above all, because it conjures up the many people who have shared memorable battles in the interest of the Italian-Canadian community: "Claire Hoy (Ottawa), William Johnson (Montreal), Angelo Persichilli (Toronto); and figures from the community such as, Lanfranco Amato, Arnalda Bartoli, Father Gianni Carparelli, Alberto Di Giovanni, Julian Gattoni, Carlo Testa, Mario Trecco, Joe Volpe." When Dan Iannuzzi died in 1994, he left behind a remarkable cultural heritage. His passing was felt with intense and deep pain by the community. In my homage to him, which appeared in the newspaper on November 23, I wrote, among other things:

> *Impartial and composed, in his judgment, Danny often took the side of the weakest member of society because he saw this as a duty on the part of the newspaper. He believed, as few do, in the safeguarding and in the spread of the Italian language and culture, always defending in the forefront and in the first person, the linguistic and cultural values of the community.*

Two years before Iannuzzi's passing we lost Johnny Lombardi: two parallel lives; two major players who were among the architects of the social and cultural revolution that has transformed Canada, turning one of the many multi-ethnic societies in the world into an authentic multi-cultural community. Raised in Toronto, Johnny Lombardi left a promising career as a musician and possible future as a journalist to join the Canadian military during the Second World War. His service saw him engaged in the decisive Allied landings in Normandy. On his return to Canada, he joined the successful family business importing Italian food products, until he finally could start the career he always desired. For 15 years Lombardi ran a program of Italian music on Chum Radio, nurturing in the meantime his most ambitious dream, which is to create his own radio station. In 1966, the dream became a reality with the founding of CHIN Radio. In the name of the radio station lies the manifesto of the station: the joy of living in the multicultural setting offered by Canada. "C" stood for Canada, "H" for happiness, and "IN" for international. Over the years, Radio CHIN became an empire, with popular radio programs in Italian and another 30 languages; a very successful TV network; the production of concerts involving the most popular artists of the Italian scene; and also with the famous CHIN International picnic, which each year brings together tens of thousands of participants on the large island in the middle of Lake Ontario, facing the city of Toronto.

Lombardi's work was of exceptional importance within the Italian community, and even more, in giving voice and importance to all the communities of immigrants, it provided a concrete demonstration of how the concept of "Canadian Mosaic" should be properly understood. In his homily on March 25 of 2002, for his funeral, Father Gregory Botte rightly acknowledged this: *"Johnny realized that behind the mosaic are only pieces of broken glass. Many different colours, many different shapes, a lot of broken pieces, but put it together, it's spectacular."*

Lombardi and Iannuzzi and all those who collaborated with them, beginning with Odoardo Di Santo and Gino Fantauzzi, not to mention, Umberto Manca, Angelo Persichilli and Benito Framarin, contributed to the important role the media played in the formation of public opinion. Through the media, news was circulated and amplified, giving the Italian-Canadian community, year after year, an unparalleled increase in prestige and power within the nation. In addition to those I mentioned above, I would like to recall the contributions of other highly professional journalists and writers of the Italian-Canadian community: notably, Antonio Nicaso, author of several books on organized crime, and Antonio Maglio; also sportswriters such as Tino Baxa, Nicola Sparano and Paolo Canciani. The latter was also a keen observer of community events, first with Fantauzzi's Multilingual Television station, then with Telelatino, and finally with CHIN Radio.

In the early years, Lombardi and Iannuzzi found themselves supporting the "Notables," probably because they were receiving financial support. At a certain point, they also tried to join the ranks of the "notables"; however, it did not take them long to realize that times were changing. Little by little their orientation changed and became markedly more progressive, as they became aware of the true needs of the majority of Italian Canadians. Soon they both realized they would have to leave the "Notables" to their fate, and instead give space and testimony to the voices coming from below. From the beginning, they had engaged in a fierce competition, mainly because he who managed to gain the biggest audience would realize higher profits, especially with advertising revenue. In the end, the competition became a battle for who could best serve the interests of the community. Both men played a distinctive role in removing excessive and unwarranted power from the "Notables" and in enhancing, instead, the role and initiatives of the trade union movement.

Particularly memorable was the struggle for a Workmen's Compensation Board, so that through its institution, it might come to provide appropriate assistance to workers affected by disability. It should be noted that most workplace accidents involved Italians, and that the *Corriere*, traditionally conservative, did not hesitate to openly take sides against the Conservative Government, which had been engaged in bitterly opposing that valuable social innovation.

These were extremely difficult battles to fight, partly because the Anglophone sector of the trade unions did not take kindly to immigrants in general, and to Italians in particular: "They take our work from us, by taking less pay." In fact, as always and everywhere, immigrants were subjected to serious exploitation by businesses: low wages, long hours, nonexistent safety and social security. The exploitation of them and their poor living conditions were the main reasons for the accidents, which not by chance, particularly occurred to Italians who worked with competence and productivity well above average and led very Spartan lives, dedicated primarily to sending money to their families far away.

The struggle for insurance against accidents at work became a topic of general interest, as well as a powerful success factor for the establishment of the Workmen's Compensation Board. It was also thanks to an initiative to which few had initially attributed more value than the usual student antics: a pantomime staged during the traditional picnic on Centre Island on Lake Ontario, organized by the *Corriere Canadese* that year, in 1970. The highlight of that community gathering, contrary to the usual beauty contest or final big plate of spaghetti, was the pantomime dedicated to safety in the workplace. The inspiration for the show was the outrageous sentence by a judge, who, in order to exonerate from any liability the employer, had found nothing better than to attribute to the wind the cause of serious injury to three workers who were victims. The news of the unusual and emotional presentation revealed the importance of this dramatic issue, seizing space and prominence on all media.

With the death of Lombardi, everyone suddenly realized the loss of a great communicator, enormously popular, and at the same time, egalitarian. His was a simple language, composed of a mixture of English and Italian dialects, but the content was always full of exemplary wisdom. Two of his many memorable phrases still pop up in conversations: "*Avete fatte'na bona giobba!*" (You've done a good job!) and "*Parlate poco, ma dicite assai!*" (Speak little, but say much!). Johnny passed the baton to his son, Lenny, who was ready to manage his father's legacy on the administrative level, such as programming, with an approach that constantly adapts to the changing times.

Much different would be the future of the *Corriere Canadese*. Iannuzzi was a sophisticated individual, as far as both language and ideas. "Proudly Italian, fiercely Canadian," was his motto and a concept of life which had inspired an entire generation. It was not rhetorical in the least, but a realistic way of interpreting Canadian society in its constitutive multi-ethnicity. Unfortunately, with the passing of Iannuzzi no one knew how to cultivate that message. While continuing to arrive punctually at newsstands, the *Corriere Canadese* had lost its identity, also it seems, because of the constraints imposed by the financial support of the Italian government. It was a difficult business to carry on for the post-Iannuzzi paper. In the past the *Corriere* had been able to overcome trials no less difficult, even though, in those circumstances, the genius of Iannuzzi had been the decisive factor in always being able to come up with something to overcome obstacles and to make things even better than before. The inevitable was announced on May 4, 2013 with a terse press release announcing the suspension of publications. With those few words, after more than half a century the book seemed to close permanently on a glorious page in the history of Italian Canadians. But miracles still happen! A few months later, to everyone's surprise, the *Corriere* was taken over by a group headed by the former Parliamentarian Joe Volpe. So far, the new editorial team made up of Joe Volpe, editor, Franco Veronesi, director, and veteran journalist Nicola Sparano, vice-director, has been able to re-establish the same authoritative voice and prestige as previously held by the paper. The series of investigative reports on community affairs, particularly on the restrictive immigration policies of the present federal government, continues the tradition of outspoken advocacy on behalf of the community. The attitude of the new *Corriere* has been innovative and culturally and politically open.

If, for Italians in Toronto, Iannuzzi and Lombardi were the main protagonists in the world of the media, there were certainly attempts to give substance to alternative voices. As far as publications in print, the initiatives have been numerous, but none of them has managed to establish itself permanently, save one: *Lo Specchio*. Founded in 1984 as a monthly by Sergio Tagliavini who had previously gained experience at the *Corriere Canadese*, the newspaper immediately took off on a biweekly basis, and then later became a weekly. *Lo Specchio* was born as a periodical to serve specific local communities such as North York and York, and later established itself as an important voice in the community located north of Toronto, that is, Vaughan, where it is distributed free to approximately 18,000 families.

Tagliavini and his business partner Giovanna Tozzi distinguished themselves also as being the promoters of two major community initiatives: the creation of a monument to the fallen Italian labourers, which was erected at the intersection of Highway 7 and Islington Avenue; and the organization, ongoing now for a quarter of a century, of the Woodbridge Festival.

In television, one cannot overlook the contribution of Emilio Mascia, a native of Molise. His debut came in the pioneering days of the 60s and 70s, with a half-hour Sunday program on Channel 22 in Hamilton. The program, in the format of a newscast covering the local, national and international scene, devoted significant attention to sporting events and was hugely popular. At the height of success, instead of adhering to the requests for extension of the program aired from Hamilton, Mascia embraced an undertaking of far more extensive commitment: after obtaining a license for a channel devoted entirely to Italian and Spanish, Mascia created Telelatino. The early years were marked by great success, but then, with the departure of Mascia and the activation of RAI International, the Telelatino programs were emptied of their original social and community content, ending up being almost irrelevant to the Italian-Canadian community. RAI International was able to transmit its programming in Canada only after winning a heated battle with Telelatino and yet, it also, after a few years, lost the interest of Italian Canadians, except for fans of soccer and of transmissions based on light entertainment.

Much more attentive to the Italian-Canadian community and eagerly followed by it, has long been the Omni Channel, owned by the powerful Rogers network which had replaced Iannuzzi's Channel 47. Although it does not cover a very wide range of programs in Italian, Omni has achieved considerable success on account of its innovative and captivating style, the result of effective teamwork. Its well-balanced coverage of international, Canadian, Italian and community events is based on the principle of service television and shows excellent results. However, recent developments have been moving in the opposite direction: to our dismay, Italian language programs have been drastically reduced.

Finally, there are some recent initiatives worthy of mention. The first, Panorama, co-edited by Roberto Bandiera and Enzo Di Mauro, is aimed at the middle-aged market, with coverage of community events, clubs, and organizations. It appears in a digital format. A second, called *Panoram Italia*, is a glossy magazine published in both Montreal and Toronto. Each edition is organized around a theme, such as fashion, art, or regional traditions, with an expected readership from the younger generation. *Accenti Magazine,* also based in Montreal, has promoted a short story contest and a photo contest for ten years, as well as covering Italian Canadian items of interest across Canada.

FIFTEEN

Italian Theatre in Toronto

THEATRE IN ITALY has been, for centuries, one of the major expressions of popular culture, a form of entertainment which appealed to the masses, to the aristocracy, and to the emerging middle classes. While plays began in churches as sacred presentations, there were also lively street performances of *commedia dell'arte*, and one can't overlook the development of opera throughout the 19th century. Every small town had some type of amateur theatre group performing plays to enthusiastic audiences. It was no surprise that theatre was a tradition the Italian immigrants brought with them to Canada. References are made to Italian language theatre in Toronto with the arrival of James Formeri, in 1853, as the founder of the Modern Languages Department at King's College, which later became the University of Toronto.

References are made also to theatre activities in Italian shortly after World War I, but it isn't until after the Second World War that we have satisfactory documentation of the presence of theatrical companies in Toronto, organized around parish churches that served the Italian-speaking newcomers. The first such amateur company was the Filodrammatica Juventus Fervida, at St. Mary of the Angels Church on Dufferin St. The second known club was the Filodrammatica of St. Agnes Church, also in the west end of Toronto. Parish churches were the natural gathering places for the first wave of post-war immigrants, where families could socialize and find some cultural expression. The first major production by the Filodrammatica of St. Agnes Church took place on May 6, 1951, with Eduardo De Filippo's brilliant comedy, *Non ti pago*, directed by Ontario Sarracini. With his eloquent voice, Sarracini was a popular radio announcer who also pioneered the first Italian language television show, one half-hour weekly. Bruno Mesaglio, who arrived in 1949, played the lead role in *Non ti pago*, and the cast included other individuals who would soon form the core of actors in Italian language productions for years to come. The cast included: Flavia Morandi, Aurora Bartolini, Moreno Danesi, Domenico and Vito Bartolini, Edda Danesi, Ada Martini, and Bruno Mesaglio's wife, Elena.

Bruno Mesaglio was a charismatic personality who not only loved theatre himself, but was able to transmit his passion to motivate others to create a dynamic group capable of putting on plays of remarkable quality. His talent attracted players from many other amateur groups. The new Piccolo Teatro Italiano was headquartered in the Italian Canadian Recreation Club on Brandon Avenue. The company ultimately included: Luigi Sartori, Luigi Zorzelli, Dedena Morello, Maria Luisa Pecota, Alberto De Rosa, Tino Baxa, Roberto Milanesi, Gino Speca, Bruno Carlesimo, Giorgio Petta, and Joe Garibaldi. Giovanni Grohovaz, a respected journalist and manager of the Italian Canadian Recreation Club, gives a first-hand account of the activities of the Piccolo Teatro from 1950 to 1970, in an article published in Polyphony, the bulletin of the Multicultural History Society of Ontario, Vol. 5, no. 2, Winter, 1983.

The first notable play produced by the Piccolo Teatro, was *l'Aqua Cheta* by Novelli, in 1952, which played to full houses, and even earned a two-column review by Eric Geiger in the *Toronto Telegram*. For the next five years the Piccolo Teatro mounted popular, entertaining plays which always attracted big audiences in the rapidly-growing Italian population of Toronto. Bruno Mesaglio was invited to direct plays at the University of Toronto for students of the Italian language courses. Then, in 1957, to celebrate the 250th anniversary of the birth of Italian playwright Carlo Goldoni, Maestro Mesaglio felt prepared to direct *La Locandiera*. The play opened on November 17, 1957, representing a milestone for Italian language cultural events in Canada. Goldoni's theatrical heritage runs deep; only De Filippo and Pirandello can compete with the quality of this repertoire. The *Corriere Canadese* writer Giuseppe Menasse penned an enthusiastic review. The production of *La Locandiera* was repeated at the Pylon Theatre in December, and word of the success reached Italy, covered by the weekly *Il Tempo di Milano*. After this peak, the choices of plays returned to the light entertainment of previous years.

By 1960, Toronto's Piccolo Teatro was capable of attracting a large audience to every performance. After a touring visit by the original Piccolo Teatro di Milano, Maestro Mesaglio decided to mount another Goldoni piece, *Il Bugiardo*. It was an unprecedented success, with performances in Toronto and Hamilton. A long article written by Walter Kanitz for the *Toronto Star* praised the production, claiming it was worthy of an award by the Dominion Drama Festival, except that the play was not in English or French. The Piccolo Teatro did receive a special award from Venice, for contribution to the works of Goldoni. This period was the high point for the director and the actors of this community theatre company. In the Polyphony article cited earlier, Gianni Grohovaz relates the involvement of three members of the Piccolo Teatro corps in a made-for-television film of Henry James' *The Aspen Papers*. Bruno Mesaglio, Luigi Zorzella, and Alberto De Rosa acted in English, and after this were able to find professional work in commercials and other Canadian television shows. Annual productions continued throughout the decade. New actors joined the company, including Marcello Danesi, Teresa Patullo, Franco Spezzano, and Vittorio Torchia for the 1966 production of *Buona Notte Patrizia*, a comedy by Aldo De Benedetti.

As the Piccolo Teatro continued to be present in the Italian cultural community, the youthful energy of the students in the Italian Club at the University of Toronto began to emerge. These young people were the first generation of children born to the post-war immigrants. Their presence on the St. George campus of the University of Toronto brought about a rapid increase in the Italian language undergraduate courses, and their enthusiasm contributed to a vibrant Italian Club on campus, especially at St. Michael's College. Plays put on by the Italian Club were performed at Hart House Theatre, the prestigious stage built into Hart House when the Massey family donated the building to the University as a student centre. In 1954, the Italian Club had produced *Scampolo*, by Niccodemi; in 1958, it was the popular *Addio giovinezza* by Camasio and Oxilia; in 1961, Veneziano's *L'antenato*; *La zia di Carlo* by Oscar Wilde, in 1962. Other productions included Chiarelli's *La maschera e il volto* (Dec., 1962), *Roxy*, by Connors (Jan., 1964), Goldoni's *Gli inna-morati* (Dec., 1964), and *La locandiera* (Dec., 1965), and Pirandello's *Enrico IV* (Dec., 1966). The list goes on, entertaining plays well-supported by the Italian community. Maestro Mesaglio imparted his knowledge of acting skills and stagecraft to Susan Scotti, Guido Pugliese, Madeleine Manella, Alessandro Gualtieri, Victor Gallo, Anna Strever, Mauro Cotechini, Agostino Settecase, Paolo Siraco, Teresa Patullo, and Carmen Nepa. This experience gave many undergraduates their first experience in community participation and built their confidence for future leadership roles. Carmen Nepa and Mauro Cotechini stood out for their exceptional talent.

Among the student cast members at the end of the decade appear several young actors who would go on to form the semi-professional Italian language theatre group, the Compagnia dei Giovani. *Addio gio-vinezza (1968)*, *Come le foglie (1969)*, and *Qualcosa comunque (1970)* represented an embryonic stage of the Compagnia dei Giovani. These plays marked the transition from university theatre to community theatre. The founders of the new entity included Alberto Di Giovanni, Celestino De Iuliis, the brothers Damiano and Domenico Pietropaolo, Maria Mancuso, Anna Cautilli, and Marielle Bertelli. They recognized the opportunity to move outward from the academic setting, while at the same time selecting plays with more literary impact than pure entertainment. The first production of the Compagnia dei Giovani took place at Hart House Theatre in March, 1971. Goldoni's *La Locandiera* was directed by Bruno Mesaglio, with Alberto Di Giovanni as the producer, a new position that established the distinct change from reliance on either the university or the Piccolo Teatro. The cast of this first production included Carmen Nepa, the Pietropaolo brothers Damiano and Domenico, Mariella Bertelli, Anna Cautilli, Maria Mancuso, Celestino De Iuliis, and Lorenzo Dragonieri.

After this success, the Compagnia dei Giovani parted amicably with Bruno Mesaglio, and undertook to establish a presence in the larger Toronto community, with a new approach to productions. They wanted their plays to reflect the Italian theatre tradition, including the opportunity to explore contemporary texts as well as the classics. New members were recruited, including Tonia Serrao, Enza Gallo, Laura Springolo, Nivo Angeloni, Domingo Spano, Joe Garibaldi, and Franco Pagliaro. In November, 1972, they performed Nicolo Machiavelli's *La Mandragola*, at the St. Lawrence Centre on Front St., as part of the inaugural Ontario Multicultural Theatre Festival. They also brought this into the community in December, 1972, at Vaughan Road Collegiate. In April, 1973, the adventurous Compagnia presented the first production in Toronto of a play by Dario Fo, *L'uomo nudo e l'uomo in frak,* featuring Damiano Pietropaolo, who later became a producer of the Ideas program on CBC Radio. This one-act play was matched with a one-act Pirandello play, *La patente.* In November, 1973, for the second Multicultural Theatre Festival, the Compagnia presented the Ugo Betti masterpiece, *La Regina e gli Insorti,* directed by Damiano Pietropaolo, with the leading role played by Tonia Serrao. The play received rave reviews in both the Italian and the English language media.

The Multicultural Theatre Festival was created by the Multicultural Theatre Association of Ontario, an umbrella organization started in 1971 to bring together ethnic theatre groups putting on plays in each community's language. By working together, they sought access to the resources of the civic stages in Toronto. More importantly, they would be able to demonstrate to the Toronto population the high quality of some of the theatre talent in the city, performing in languages other than English or French. I was the first president to be elected, and

I remained active within the Association for the next 10 years. The Multicultural Theatre Association enabled its member companies to travel and bring their plays to festivals around the country. In 1975, the Compagnia revived its production of *La Locandiera* by Goldoni, and brought it to the National Multicultural Theatre Festival held in the Grand Théatre du Québec, in Quebec City. This play also toured to Montreal and Toronto.

The Piccolo Teatro company had ceased productions by 1971; however, its influence was still present in the community, particularly among the actors. In 1975, I approached the actors of both the Piccolo Teatro and the Compagnia dei Giovani, and suggested that together we pay tribute to Maestro Mesaglio with a distinctive production. The reaction was enthusiastic. We chose to do Luigi Pirandello's great play, *Cosi é (se vi pare)*. After that, as producer of the Compagnia dei Giovani, I called on Maestro Mesaglio and invited him to direct this challenging masterpiece. The result was an astounding success, eliciting warm media coverage and something of a hero's welcome by audiences. The Pirandello play took the stage at St. Lawrence Centre in November, 1976, as part of the fifth annual Multicultural Theatre Festival. This production was repeated several times in community locations, always commanding a full house and standing ovations. Bringing the two groups together in performance worked brilliantly, but this was never to be repeated. Bruno Mesaglio, director, actor, mentor, and friend, passed away on April 11, 1977.

In 1978, the Compagnia mounted two one-act plays by Luigi Pirandello, as part of the annual Multicultural Theatre Festival in Toronto. *Cecé* was directed by Damiano Pietropaolo, and *L'uomo dal fiore in bocca*, directed by Mariella Bertelli. They received a total of seven awards from the Festival adjudicators: Best Festival Performance, presented to producer Alberto Di Giovanni; Best Director to Damiano Pietropaolo and Mariella Bertelli, jointly; both also received the awards as Best Actor and Best Actress in Leading Roles; Franco Pagliaro received the adjudicator's Special Mention; and Laura Springolo, Best Visual Presentation Award for set design. As winner of the top performance prize, the Compagnia represented Ontario at the National Multicultural Theatre Festival in Windsor, Ontario in July, 1979. Before that, in December, 1978, an English version of *Cecé* was presented at the Fifth International Congress on Pirandello, in Agrigento, Italy. After this, at the initiative of the producer, Di Giovanni, the Compagnia made several appearances in Italy. In 1979, three Compagnia members: De Iuliis, Bertelli, and Springolo, translated into Italian the play *A toi, pour toujours, Marie-Lou* by acclaimed Quebec writer Michel Tremblay. This was first performed at Hart House on March 9 and 10, 1979, and then in the Teatro Goldoni in Rome, on March 19 to 22, 1979, supported by the Canadian Embassy in Rome. The Roman performances were favourably reviewed by both *Paese Sera* and the *Daily American*. Subsequently, in May, 1979, the play was repeated at the National Multicultural Theatre Festival in Oakville, Ontario.

For the eighth annual Multicultural Theatre Festival, in November, 1979, the Compagnia dei Giovani presented Pirandello`s charming *Ma non é una cosa seria*, directed by Damiano Pietropaolo. Shortly after that performance, in December, 1979, the play was brought to the Sixth International Congress on Pirandello in Italy. In November, 1980, for the ninth annual Multicultural Theatre Festival, the Compagnia dei Giovani again presented two one-act plays, *Solange*, by Jean Barbeau, and *L'uomo nudo e l'uomo in frak*, by Dario Fo. At this point, after more than 10 years together putting on excellent productions in Italian and occasionally in English, the members of the Compagnia dei Giovani moved on with their professional lives, finding it difficult to devote so many hours as volunteers in a cultural endeavour they loved and gladly contributed to their shared Italian community heritage.

Student productions of plays in Italian continued to be performed by the Italian Clubs at the St. George campus, University of Toronto, and with special vigour at the Erindale U of T campus, under the guidance of Guido Pugliese, Luciana Marchionne, and Salvatore Bancheri.

Three other theatrical groups contributed to the appreciation of performance art in the wider community. Edu-Art, coordinated by Franco Spezzano and Cosmo Barranca, operated with federal government support in 1973, bringing performers into community settings for adults and youth. Pinocchio on the Road, a summer Local Initiative Project, acted out folk tales and stories in English and Italian, in playgrounds, community centres, and schools. This was coordinated by Caroline Morgan Di Giovanni, with actors from the Compagnia dei Giovani. Deserving of special mention was Teatro Italiano dell'Arte, which performed from 1973 to 1976, under the direction of Fulvio Marchi.

Two other events featuring Italian performers visiting Toronto left a lasting impression on the emerging cultural life of the city and the Italian community. In 1964, to celebrate "100 Years of Settlement in Canada," the Italian Canadian Recreation Club hosted a dinner to honour the touring company that performed the Roman musical, *Rugantino*. The starring cast members included the famous Nino Manfredi, Ornella Vanoni, and Aldo Fabrizi, some of the most successful Italian stage and film actors, known around the world.

I wish to close this chapter on Italian theatre in Toronto with a description of the outstanding participation of the Teatro Stabile dell'Aquila in the first Toronto International Theatre Festival, in the spring of 1981. As Director of Centro Scuola e Cultura Italiana, I contacted the group to make arrangements for this new initiative. The Teatro Stabile, directed by Antonio Calenda, presented *La Passione*, a medieval passion play in an archaic dialect, with costumes based on the Nazi occupation in World War II. Featuring the great Elsa Merlini as the Madonna, the play had been put on in major cathedrals in Italy. For the Toronto festival, the location was the hockey arena at St. Michael's College School. All five performances in Toronto were completely sold out, as were the productions in Thorold and in Ottawa, reaching a total audience of 7000 patrons. The *Passione* was judged by the critics as the best show of the festival, among productions from all around the globe. It achieved rave reviews in media across Canada. Carole Corbeil wrote in the *Globe and Mail*: "Italy's stunning *Passione* is a breathtaking triumph." This was echoed by Gina Mallet in the *Toronto Star*, calling the *Passione* "enchanting theatre...A production with a huge

144

emotional impact." John Hare, in the *Ottawa Citizen*, headlined "Italian troupe offers rare theatre brilliance." Critical praise also poured in from *The London Times, The Montreal Gazette,* and *Maclean's Magazine.* The *Corriere Canadese* reviews were so notable that several national newspapers in Italy also reported on the astonishing success of the Canadian tour. Reminiscing on this experience still gives me goose bumps.

SIXTEEN

Italian Canadians
in the Canadian Culture

ITALIAN CANADIANS have gained prominent roles in all aspects of Canadian cultural life. Artists, writers, actors, musicians, and film makers with Italian names appear in programmes and on posters regularly. In this chapter, I can present only a few of the individuals who are contributing to the arts and letters from coast to coast. The cultural presence of Italian Canadians has obviously asserted itself in all fields, from music to plastic and figurative arts, from theatre to cinema, from architecture to design, giving rise to such a variety of expressions that by now it would be extremely difficult to attempt listing them all.

Early on, the painter Joe Cusimano, an artist from the school of De Chirico, made his mark with many distinctive works. Joe Catalano, a third-generation Italian Canadian, studied at the Ontario College of Art and Design. He founded the Toronto ad agency, *Concept 3*, where his work as an artist and graphic designer has garnered fame and numerous awards throughout North America. In the 1970s, Silvio Mastrodascio moved to Toronto from his home in Teramo, where he had graduated *cum laude* in sculpture from the College of Fine Arts. Talent and skill has brought him success not only in Canada, but also in Italy, Japan, the US, South America, and Europe. In Toronto his works include the bronze bezel on the rear door of the Cathedral, and two large sculptures commissioned by the Bell Mobility Centre for its head office. Albert Chiarandini came to Canada from Udine in 1938, and at the young age of 23 organized his first art exhibit here. It was well received by the critics, foreshadowing a lengthy career with an output of more than 3,000 paintings, shown in many North American galleries, including the Art Gallery of Toronto (now the AGO). In 1960, he was honoured by recognition as a Fellow of the Federation of International Institutes of Arts and Letters (FIIAL).

One of the most successful of the Italian-Canadian painters before the millennium was Luigi Bellini, whose paintings of City Hall, Toronto in the 1940s, and other urban scenes, can be found in the homes of art patrons all over the Greater Toronto Area. Artist Francesca Vivenza, a graduate of the Accademia Brera in Milan, enjoys a bright reputation for her contemporary drawings and, in particular, installations. Photography as an art form and a documentary record has been the passion of Vincenzo Pietropaolo. His black-and-white images of workers on the job capture the sweat and toil of many Italian-Canadian immigrants.

The presence of Italian-Canadian writers in Canadian circles has grown exponentially since the first short stories and poems appeared in journals in the 1970s. The characters in the stories by Dino Minni, set in Vancouver, were distinctly identified as Italian Canadians. In 1978, poet Pier Giorgio Di Cicco, acting as mentor, editor, and big brother, gathered the poetry of 17 young writers into the ground breaking anthology, *Roman Candles*. Following this, in 1984, the first edition of *Italian Canadian Voices: an Anthology of Poetry and Prose (1946-1983)* was published, edited by Caroline Morgan Di Giovanni, and supported by Centro Scuola. This volume contained the first English version of Mario Duliani's account of life in the internment camp at Petawawa. It also contained excerpts from Frank Paci's novel, *Black Madonna*, and from Caterina Edwards' novel, *The Lion's Mouth*. Many of the writers in this collection formed the Association of Italian Canadian Writers after a conference held in 1986. That association, and its members, continue to produce long form fiction, short stories, and poetry reflecting their roots and heritage while earning recognition as important Canadian authors. In 1998, Joseph Pivato edited *The Anthology of Italian Canadian Writers,* a collection that included not only creative writing but also some essays of astute critical analysis. There is also an anthology of women writers, *Pillars of Lace,* edited by Delia De Santis; two editions of *Sweet Lemons,* edited by De Santis and Venera Fazio; a revised version of *Italian Canadian Voices,* in 2006, and *Bravo! A Selection of Prose and Poetry by Italian Canadian Writers,* edited by Caroline M. Di Giovanni, in 2012. These anthologies exhibit the wide variety of writers who have grown up in two worlds, bringing the warmth of the Mediterranean into the cool Canadian climate. As Prof. Vera Golini writes in her essay, Why a New Anthology of Italian Canadian Voices, "the works...illustrate to what extent the person and the human condition are the focal subjects of much Italian Canadian writing over the past six decades." (p. 210, *Italian Canadian Voices,* 2006.)

These specific characteristics were the elements which brought the success that Italian-Canadian authors have obtained in the context of Canadian literature, earning prestige and popularity. Nino Ricci's most successful novel, *Lives of the Saints,* won the Governor General's Award for Literature in English, in 1990, and continues to collect prizes and reprints. Pier Giorgio Di Cicco served as the Poet Laureate of Toronto, 2004-2009. He had written more than 17 books of poems before entering the priesthood; after ordination, he continued to publish poetry, as well as essays on modern life. Nino Ricci won a second Governor General's Award in 2008, for *The Origin of Species.* While these two men have gained major prominence in the literary scene, they are not unique. There have emerged, among others, refined poets such as Mary Di Michele , Gianna Patriarca, Len Gasparini, George Amabile , Saro D'Agostino, and fascinating prose writers such as Frank G. Paci, Darlene Madott, John Calabro, Caterina Edwards, and Michael Mirolla. In the case of Antonino Mazza, an exquisite poet and prose writer, he distinguished himself for his excellent English version of the extremely challenging poems by Eugenio Montale.

The multi-faceted personality of Calogero (Charly) Chiarelli is the focus of attention in the entertainment world. Hailing from Sicily at an early age, Charly grew up in the industrial area of Hamilton, later receiving a degree in psychology, linguistics and sociology at the universities of Carleton, McMaster and Toronto. He extended his professional social work career by becoming a popular actor and musician. His monologues *Cu'Fu*, *Mangiacake* and *Brutta Figura* assured him success and fame, not only for his theatrical performances that are much in demand, but also due to screenings of television shows.

And what can one say about Antoni Cimolino? After many years acting and directing in dozens of productions of the great Shakespearean classics, Cimolino has reached the top spot of the Stratford Shakespeare Festival in Ontario, the most famous and important theatre festival dedicated to Shakespeare outside of England. Prior to assuming the duties of artistic director, Cimolino had been instrumental in the remodelling of the Festival, radically changing its soul and structure. Not surprisingly, he is presented in official publications published by the Festival in 2013 thus: "Now in his 26th season at the Festival, Mr. Cimolino is a respected artist and an influential leader and visionary worldwide."

The world of the theatre is full of the presence of Italians and offers some influential names among great actors recognized on the Canadian stage, screen, and television. There was Bruno Gerussi, well-known from the popular *Beachcombers* series. Jennifer Dale worked with Nick Mancuso at Tarragon Theatre in a play about Eleanora Duse. Mancuso made shows in Los Angeles before returning to Toronto, where he co-starred with Sophia Loren in a film version of *Lives of the Saints*. Tony Nardi made the film *Quasi America* with Sabrina Ferilli. He also made a name for himself by writing and performing his monologues, *Two Letters* and subsequent versions of *Letters*, criticizing the stereotypes he observed in the tight knit world of the stage. Two very popular television shows have brought Italian-Canadian actors into everyone's home. *Flashpoint* starred the handsome Enrico Colantoni, and multi-talented Paula Brancati was in the cast of *De Grassi:The Next Generation*, and also in *Being Erica*.

A well-known protagonist of the cultural scene in Toronto is Tony Gagliano, recognized above all as a co-creator, together with the late David Pecaut, of Luminato, considered the largest festival of the arts in Canada. Gagliano is also a successful entrepreneur in the field of publishing and telecommunications as well as an active member of philanthropic endeavours. In his role as President of the Art Gallery of Ontario, he has among other things promoted the development of Galleria Italia, a grand space created as part of the now famous refurbishment of the museum designed by architect Frank Gehry.

Music has always constituted a major cultural interest for Italians; therefore it is natural to find some great singers and musicians within the Italian Canadian community. Ermanno Mauro, tenor, Louis Quilico, baritone, and Maria Pellegrini, soprano, all have graced the opera stages of the Metropolitan in New York, La Scala in Milan, and of course the Canadian Opera Company in Toronto. They also contributed their knowledge of the opera world as well as vocal training to hundreds of students over the years. Fame and international prestige came to Maestro Mario Bernardi, conductor of the CBC Orchestra, heard on the radio across the country, and captured on many records and CDs. Ermanno Florio also achieved distinction as conductor at La Scala. Two recent additions to the musical scene in Canada both play in the famous Tafelmusik Baroque Orchestra in Toronto. Marco Cera plays oboe, and occasionally other instruments, in this ensemble. Stefano Marcocchi, violist, joined Tafelmusik in 2014. Mention must also be made of the classically-trained singer Francesco Pellegrino, who has brought to life traditional Neapolitan songs with the very engaging Vesuvius Ensemble.

A relatively new cultural association, L'Altra Italia, was started in 2002 by Cristiano De Floriis, representative of RAI International in Canada, and Maurizio Magnifico. It began as a film club, with dinner and an opportunity for socializing. Immediately successful, L'Altra Italia can fill the cinemas in Toronto and Vaughan every month, projecting recently released Italian films. Its reputation has grown, so that now the audience is made up of equal numbers of Italians and non-Italians.

Shows have often been attended by the directors, such as Nanni Moretti and others. In 2012, L'Altra Italia launched the Italian Contemporary Film Festival, annually presenting over 50 films in late June and early July.

As a fitting conclusion to this chapter on the influence of Italian cultural heritage, I am pleased to describe the work of Professor Domenico Pietropaolo, Dante scholar and academic administrator. The first Italian Canadian to serve as Principal of St. Michael's College, University of Toronto, Professor Pietropaolo returned to his alma mater full of creative ideas. We have been friends for many years, not least of which involved our efforts with the Compagnia dei Giovani. Therefore, we seized the opportunity together to establish a special collection of Dante volumes, in facsimile manuscripts, rare illustrated editions, and critical studies, to be located in a room named the Casa Dante, within the John M. Kelly Library, the jewel of the St. Michael's campus. Certainly the visible and tangible presence of this special collection will inspire Canadian university students far into the future.

SEVENTEEN

Integration, Nationality and Citizenship

THE THEORY OF "THE MELTING POT" which was developed in the United States has long been the benchmark for policies relating to immigration issues. The "melting pot" aims at the fusion between different racial and ethnic groups, through a process of dissolution of different minorities subject to the acceptance of the socio-political and cultural conditions imposed by the dominant member. Notoriously, however, he who is assimilated runs the risk of cultural alienation. Instead, the real achievement of civilization is not in homogenizing the different groups into the dominant model. Rather, the true achievement of civilization is "nationality," that is, national identity which is the result of an historical and cultural process based on the recognition of all the social, cultural and ethnic components present in the communities and in the state organization that unifies and coordinates them, so that they might function together as a national identity, but each well-defined and distinct from the others.

Cesare Balbo clearly identified the substance of all that was achieved through the Enlightenment, as well as the results of the French Revolution and the American one, in the mid-19th century: "That which constitutes true nationality, and which leaves no state within a state, and which in a true nation fuses together diverse peoples, is the commonality of laws, of institutions, of interests, and especially the commonality to deliberate."

As we have seen, for Canada to move from the politics of integration to the construction of nationality was neither a simple undertaking nor a short journey. Within the international context, this was a rare case indeed, and one which has achieved an enviable success, even though there still remain a number of inadequacies that must be addressed. A significant factor in this success lies in having confronted head on the issue of citizenship. "Citizenship" is the legal status of the individual, consisting of a stable membership within a State, which is based on certain requirements, and which is embodied in a set of rights and duties. The work of Laurier, Pearson, Trudeau and many others developed the thinking that has made great strides towards the national identity. Despite great achievements, such as the creation of the province of Nunavut, the issue of the native Canadians underlines significant deficiencies, not to mention the unrest in some areas of the French-speaking population. Above all, there remains the increasingly important issue of managing the immigration patterns of recent years.

The dialogue regarding "cultural accommodation" touches the sensitive area of religion. The predominance of Catholics (47%) and Protestants (39%) is not bound to undergo any significant change, neither in the short nor medium term, but as the population changes, this may require careful attention. However, the case for ethnic and linguistic issues is somewhat different. Census data estimate the composition of the Canadian people as: 2% whose mother tongue is Aboriginal; 60% of English speakers; 24%, whose mother tongue is French; and 14% of other languages. Among these, the most numerous are German and Italian. The Chinese are on the verge of overtaking the Italians, however, while new groups from Eastern Europe, India, Pakistan, the Philippines and African countries are following closely.

The problematic issues of current immigration flows were addressed in 2002 in a precise, careful study by Jeffrey G. Reitz, a professor of sociology at the University of Toronto:

Although Canada shares with the United States and Australia the tradition of being a country of immigrants, its current expansionist immigration policies, and their comparative degree of success, are shaped by context, and by an institutional framework, both of which differ from both other countries in significant ways. These differences include Canada's development strategy in relation to its much larger American neighbour; its low fertility rates; its close proximity to the U.S. but geographic isolation from all other countries; its post-secondary educational system; its distinctive labour markets and other social institutions which reflect greater emphasis on collective welfare as opposed to American individualism; its dual linguistic structure and the autonomy of Quebec and other provinces; and its multicultural policies as affected by the impact of recent immigration in creating a multi-racial society. These various differences are evolving in ways that reflect both convergence and differentiation.

Consequently, Reitz's analysis arrives at the following: "The pattern of these changes, more than either convergence or differentiation in itself, is creating significant actual and potential difficulties for the continued success of Canadian immigration over time." In fact, Reitz adds: "Canada's perceived need for high levels of immigration will continue, but its success in integrating these immigrants is becoming more difficult, creating increased strain on the economy and society." In conclusion: "This raises significant issues and dilemmas which are likely to become more salient and produce important policy changes in the future."

All this stands to show that, not unlike any other community, Canada is not heaven on earth and is not exempt from the need to deal with the incessant evolution of economic and social phenomena. But, having said that, I cannot but make a positive assessment of my own experience as an Italian immigrant, and then as a Canadian citizen. I had the privilege of living the 20 years in which I accomplished the most important things in my life exactly during the most exciting 20 years of Canadian history.

In 1963, I came to Toronto from my native Roccamorice and in Ottawa the Pearson government was born. In the years that followed, Canada was able to define its own national identity, gain its independence, and become a universal model of a multicultural community. I graduated; I conceived and developed the Centro Scuola e Cultura Italiana of Toronto, while the Italian Canadians were rising to the role of protagonists in all organizations of the nation. I met and married Caroline, and we had our first children, Carlo Alberto and Franca; while, in 1982, the Patriation of the Constitution was achieved and, Annamaria, our youngest, arrived. How would I not feel lucky, happy and proud?

I have been privileged to serve the community in a number of ways, listed in the brief biography at the end of this book. I want to remember especially serving as a Member of the Board of Directors of the Public Library of the City of York, and as a member of the Commission for Human Rights of the Government of Ontario. I recall with deep emotion receiving the Distinguished Educator Award of the Ontario Institute for Studies in Education of the University of Toronto in 1997; the *Italiani nel Mondo* (Italians in the World) Award conferred upon me in 2002 in Rome, on a terrace overlooking the Monument to the Unknown Soldier; the Order of Merit of the Italian-Canadian National Congress in 2003; and the dedication of my name for the Library of the Columbus Centre. Yet, what gives me the greatest pride and gratitude is the esteem and affection with which I am always surrounded by my family and the Italian-Canadian community, and the knowledge that I have made a small but not insignificant contribution towards having my Canadian homeland better understand the honour and merit that are due to my Italian homeland.

The Canadian nation now exists, and the Italian Canadians are an integral part of it, with all of the rights and duties of citizenship and of nationality. Yet the centuries-old diversity of vision of the two major Canadian components is still not entirely resolved. The most striking proof is provided by one prominent symbol: the national anthem, adopted on July 1, 1980 but dating back exactly to a century ago. The music is the same as performed for the first time on June 24, 1880. The two official texts, however, are quite different: the French version, created for a religious association of Quebec City, verbatim to that of 1880, while the other is not the English version of the original but an independent text, created in 1908. The comparison is telling:

O Canada!	Ô Canada!
Our home and native land!	Terre de nos aïeux,
True patriot love in all thy sons command.	Ton front est ceint de fleurons glorieux!
With glowing hearts we see thee rise,	Car ton bras sait porter l'épée,
The True North strong and free!	Il sait porter la croix!
From far and wide,	Ton histoire est une épopée
O Canada, we stand on guard for thee.	Des plus brillants exploits.
God keep our land glorious and free!	Et ta valeur, de foi trempée,
O Canada, we stand on guard for thee.	Protégera nos foyers et nos droits.
O Canada, we stand on guard for thee.	Protégera nos foyers et nos doits.

The difference in the words is not necessarily a negative thing, but instead, perhaps, one can read in it the will to express once again the concept of unity in diversity upon which modern Canada bases its identity. We sing different words and different concepts, but the music blends the voices in perfect harmony. At least as far as I'm concerned, this is the lesson to draw. When we sing the Canadian anthem, in a stadium, or a banquet, or anywhere else, I am sentimentally moved by the differences around me, and I often sense the enthusiasm of the young people who alternate from French verses to English verses, as if to say: we are all equally Canadian, proud of it, whatever the heritage of each of us, whatever the adversity we come from, whatever the concerns and whatever the lurking difficulties. Then I like to indulge in a waking dream: a dream that one day we will all be able to sing together, each in the language of one's own forefathers: Inuit, English, Irish, French, Italians, Chinese, Ukrainians, Germans, Poles, Norwegians and many others. And all will be singing in unison the different words, to the rhythm of the same music, and see across the mountains and lakes of Canada the greatest dream of a humanity finally able to rejoice in the wonderful harmony and in the inexhaustible wealth that can flourish only from the peaceful coexistence of its great variety.

Bibliography

The research and documentation used in the preparation of this book was obtained principally from the archives of Centro Scuola e Cultura Italiana, Toronto; the archives of *The Toronto Star* newspaper, and of the *Corriere Canadese*; the websites of the Parliament of Canada, of the British Parliament, and of the Library of Congress of the United States of America.

In addition, the following sources were used:

Ariemma, Virginia Williams, *The story of Villa Charities*, Toronto, Villa Charities, 1997

Bagnell, Kenneth, *Canadese: A Portrait of the Italian Canadians*, Toronto, Macmillan, 1989

Balbo, Cesare, *Meditazioni storiche*, Firenze 1855

Berton, Pierre, *1967: The Last Good Year*, Toronto, Doubleday Canada, 1997

Centofanti, Errico, *Italiani nel Mondo*, L'Aquila, LaTerzaLaudomia, 2002

Colantonio, Frank, *From the Ground Up*, Toronto, Between the Lines, 1997

Ferguson, Edith, *Newcomers in transition; an experimental study project conducted by the International Institute of Metropolitan Toronto to study the relation between rural immigrants and Toronto's community services, March 1, 1962 – March 1, 1964*, Toronto, International Institute of Metropolitan Toronto, 1964

Framarin, Benito, *I cattivi pensieri di Don Smarto*, Padova, Edizioni Messaggero Padova, 1986

Gibbon, John Murray, *Canadian Mosaic; the Making of a Northern Nation*, Toronto, McClelland & Stewart, 1938

Harney, Nicholas De Maria, *Eh, paesan!: being Italian in Toronto*, Toronto-Buffalo-London, University of Toronto Press, 1998

Harney, Nicholas De Maria (ed.), *From the Shores of Hardship: Italians in Canada*, Welland, Editions Soleil, 1993

Harney, Robert F. – Scarpaci, J. Vincenza (eds.), *Little Italies in North America, 1885–1945*, Toronto, MHSO, 1981

Iacovetta, Franca, *Such Hardworking People: Italians in Postwar Toronto*, Montreal-Kingston, McGill-Queen's University Press, 1992

Glazer, Nathan – Moynihan, Daniel Patrick, *Beyond the melting pot; the Negroes, Puerto Ricans, Jews, Italians, and Irish of New York City*, Cambridge, Mass., M.I.T. Press, 1963

Molinaro Julius – Maddalena Kuitunen (eds.), *The Luminous Mosaic: Italian Cultural Organizations in Ontario*, Welland, Editions Soleil, 1993

Morgan Di Giovanni, Caroline, *Bravo! A Selection of Prose and Poetry by Italian Canadian Writers*, Toronto, Quattro Books, 2012

Morgan Di Giovanni, Caroline, *Italian Canadian Voices: A Literary Anthology, 1946–2004*, Oakville, Mosaic Press, 2006

Porter, John, *The vertical mosaic; an analysis of social class and power in Canada*, Toronto, University of Toronto Press, 1968

Rao, Fortunato, *The Lucky Emigrant*, Toronto, Multicultural History Society of Ontario, 2002

Reitz, Jeffrey G., *Immigration and Canadian nation-building in the transition to a knowledge economy*, University of Toronto, June 2002 (This paper was prepared as a contribution to *Controlling Immigration: a Global Perspective*, 2nd Edition, edited by Wayne A. Cornelius, Philip L. Martin, and James F. Hollifield, Stanford University Press. The author would like to thank Raymond Breton, Takeyuki Tsuda and Amanda Greener for helpful comments on an earlier draft, and Kimberly Thai for expert research assistance.

The author is R.F. Harney Professor of Ethnic, Immigration and
Pluralism Studies, and Professor of Sociology, at the University of
Toronto)

Rosoli, Gianfausto (ed.), *Un secolo di emigrazione italiana: 1876–1976*,
Roma, Centro Studi Emigrazione, 1978

Royal Commission on Bilingualism and Biculturalism, *Preliminary
Report*, Ottawa, Ministry of Supply and Services, 1966

Sbrocchi, Giuseppe Antonio, *L'emigrazione: come l'ho vista e come l'ho
vissuta*, New York-Ottawa-Toronto, Legas, 2005

Stefanini, Giancarlo. *Strike: La storia di un'italiano in Canada*. Edizioni
Lavoro, Roma, 2014

Sturino, Franc, *Forging the chain: Italian Emigration to North America,
1930–1980*, Toronto, Multicultural History Society of Ontario, 1990

Toppan, Marino, *The Voice of Labour*, Toronto, Marino Toppan 2004

Zucchi, John, *Italians in Toronto: Development of a National Identity,
1875–1935*, Montreal-Kingston, McGill-Queen's University Press,
1988

Alberto Di Giovanni: Biography

ALBERTO DI GIOVANNI was born in Roccamorice (Pescara) in the Region of Abruzzo, on June 22, 1945. He attended the classical lyceum in Chieti until 1963, when he left Italy to join his family in Canada. He attended the University of Toronto, St. Michael's College, graduating with an Hons. B.A. in Political Science and Languages in 1971, and subsequently earned a Master's Degree in Italian Language and Literature, in 1973.

Throughout his life in Canada he has been able to witness first-hand the principal events in the Italian-Canadian community for the second half of the 20th century and the start of the new millennium. He was among the founders of the Federation of Italian Canadian Associations and Clubs (FACI), and he was a founding member of the National Congress of Italian Canadians. He was a member of the General Council of Italians Abroad (2004-2014), and served as president of many cultural organizations, such as the Italian Club at the University of Toronto; the Dante Alighieri Society of Toronto, serving as Vice President of the Dante Society of North America; founding President of the Multicultural Theatre Association of Ontario; Metro Communities for International Languages; and Secretary-Treasurer of the Multicultural History Society of Ontario.

In 1976 he founded the Centro Scuola e Cultura Italiana/The Canadian Centre for Italian Culture and Education, an institution to promote Italian language through education and cultural programs.

He has contributed to diverse publications in both Italy and Canada. His constant stream of activities in the fields of culture, education, and social change earned him a place on the Library Board of the City of York, as well as on the Human Rights Commission of the Province of Ontario. He has received numerous awards and recognition such as the titles of Commendatore and Grand Ufficiale of the Order of Merit of the Italian Republic; the Queen's Golden Jubilee Medal from HR Queen Elizabeth II of the United Kingdom; the Distinguished Educator Award from the Ontario Institute for Studies in Education, University of Toronto; The Beata Beatrix Gold Medal from a Dante research centre; the Gold Star for sport activities, from the Italian National Olympic Committee; the Premio Italiani nel Mondo; the title of Ambassador of Abruzzo to the World; honorary citizen of Atri (Abruzzo) and honorary citizen of Amherstburg (Ontario). In addition, the library at the Columbus Centre in Toronto bears his name. In November, 2014, he received the designation of Honorary Fellow from the University of St. Michael's College, University of Toronto.

RECYCLED
Paper made from
recycled material
FSC® C100212

Printed in February 2015
by Gauvin Press,
Gatineau, Québec